Not just what to do, but how to do it!

ACTION PLAN FOR SALES MANAGEMENT SUCCESS

SUSAN A. ENNS

MANAGING PARTNER
B2B SALES CONNECTIONS

ISBN: 978-0-9876928-1-8

DEDICATION

To John Noble - You gave me the belief in myself that I could be successful and then you showed me how. I can still hear your Scottish accent ringing in my ear saying, "Once you have done it once, no one can tell you that you can't do it again!"

Action Plan For Sales Management Success

TABLE OF CONTENTS

Chapter 2 – Eagles or Turkeys?
Recruiting and Hiring
The Right Sales Professional 39

Chapter 4 – You Are The Coach!

"Success is simple.
 Do what's right, the right way,
 at the right time." – Arnold Glascow

INTRODUCTION

Congratulations! By purchasing *"Action Plan For Sales Management Success"* you have taken your next step towards achieving your sales potential, as well as that of your sales team! Before we get started, a little about why we are here.

Studies show 25% of sales reps produce 90 to 95% of all sales. Clearly, most sales people are not selling up to their potential, and not making the incomes they could, nor producing the revenues they should.

Why is this case? It's not that the job can't be done because 25 percent are doing it, and doing it well. It's because the other 75 percent either are not in the right sales position or they truly don't know how to sell. If all sales people knew and did what the top 25 percent do, then all sales people would be selling more!

B2B Sales Connections wants to change that. We are an online sales training website with free sales resources, a specialized sales job board and free resume listing services for business to business sales. I guess one could say we specialize in helping b2b sales professionals achieve their sales potential, either by connecting them to the right career choices, or the right skill set. Our website is b2bsalesconnections.com.

My name is Susan A. Enns, and I am Managing Partner of B2B Sales Connections. I have over 22 years of direct sales, management and executive level business to business experience. My accomplishments include being the top sales rep in Canada twice before being promoted to management, managing the top sales branch in the country, and achieving outstanding sales growth in a national channel sales organization. I have written training courses on sales and sales management, created numerous automated sales tools, and my work has been published in several locations numerous times.   I am also currently the President for the Sales Professionals of Ottawa.

The reason for me telling you this is not to toot my own horn. It's just to prove that if I can do it, anyone can! My sales success was not because I am smarter than anyone else. Mind you I have four brothers. If you ever meet them, I will deny I said that.

It was also not because I worked harder than everyone else. True, I did come from a farming family and you do learn a hard work ethic in that environment. The only way you get out of work is if there is an amputation and even then it's only when the bleeding stops. But in reality, most days I had a 5:30 tee off time so my success was not because of super long hours of work.

In reality, my success, like the rest of the sales reps in that top 25% is because I learned how to work smarter, not harder. Someone showed me the right way to do things, and I hope to help you do the same.

"Action Plan For Sales Management Success" is based on over 50 years of successful B2B sales and sales management expertise. It includes my own personal sales techniques, as well as other successful sales professionals I have been lucky enough to work with over the years.

This is not just a "30,000 foot level" discussion about what to do to sell more and manage better. More importantly, this is an action based exercise that will actually show you how! *"Action Plan For Sales Management Success"* is separated into four sections, each discussing a different function of sales management. In each section, we use of specific sales tools and templates. Manual versions of these tools are included here in the appendices located at the end of each section. If you would like to download the automated versions of the tools, you can purchase them in our eStore at www.b2bsalesconnections.com

Together we can all achieve our sales potential! So lets' get started!

Chapter 1 – The B2B Sales Process
The Sales Manager's Role

"I have more fun and enjoy more financial success
when I stop trying to get what I want and start helping
other people get what they want."
– Spencer Johnson, M.D. and Larry Wilson

THE ROLE OF THE B2B SALES MANAGER

Simply stated, the role of any sales manager is to meet or exceed the assigned objectives while working with the available resources. Different sales managers have different objectives, with some based on sale revenues, and others based on profits. The resources available also vary, from the size and structure of the sales teams, to the size of the marketing and training budgets.

Every company is unique, and therefore every sales manager's specific objectives are different. Regardless of the specifics, the importance of the sales manager's job function cannot be understated. The sales force drives the company's revenue and it the sales manager's job to drive the sales force.

If the person who is handling the sales manager's job function does not perform, the company does not generate cash, and the company does not survive! This is why many consider sales to be the most important function with any company.

Although the role of a sales manager may be easily defined, and its importance to the organization clearly understood, the skills required to be a successful sales manager are not. In many companies the business owner wears many hats, one of which happens to be the sales manager. In other organizations, the job of the sales manager was given to the sales person who previously had the highest sales results.

The problem is that most of the time the business owner or the newly promoted sales manager may not have had any practical training on how to manage a sales team properly. Without the proper training, they do not possess the necessary skills or tools required to manage this critical business function successfully.

Over and above the learned skills however, it is important to note that successful managers, those that really move the organization forward, all practice their profession while holding two beliefs:

- They know that their job is to "show how, not do for".
- They know that they will be more successful if they help others get to where they want to go, as opposed to only focusing on where they want to go.

Successful sales managers understand they will be more successful when they work through and with other people, namely their sales team. They know their personal selling abilities, but they also know that they will be more successful if they teach a team to sell as opposed to doing it themselves.

Successful sales managers also believe in exceptional customer service, and they know the more successful their customers are, the more successful they will be. The key is they realize that their customers are actually their sales teams!

Pictured below is a standard organizational chart, with the highest ranking company official of the company at the top. The reporting structure filters down through the sales department to the customer.

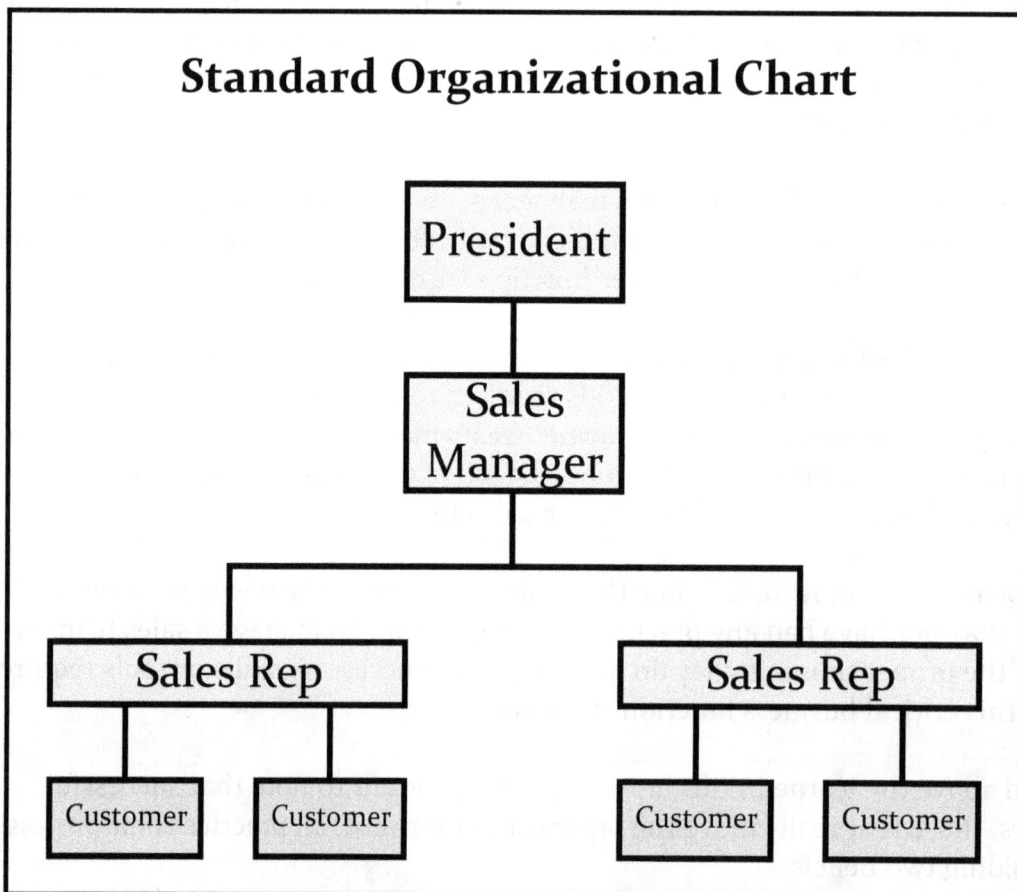

Standard Organizational Chart

```
                    President
                        |
                  Sales Manager
                        |
         +--------------+--------------+
     Sales Rep                     Sales Rep
         |                             |
    +----+----+                   +----+----+
 Customer  Customer           Customer  Customer
```

Thinking of a sales organization this way truly creates a "keep the boss happy" attitude. The sales manager is concerned with the sales results because that is what the boss keeps pushing for. The manager then drives the sales representatives to do the same, who in turn pushes the customers to buy more products. The end result typically is that the sales reps are pushed to sell more because that is what their manager wants, not because that is what the customers want.

In reality, however, it is the customers of an organization that should be at the top. They are the ones who ultimately must be kept happy if the organization is to be successful, not the boss. When thought of this way, the sales representatives report to the customers, with their prime responsibility becoming keeping them happy as opposed to their sales manager.

In other words, a sales manager must think of the organization in reverse. The happier he keeps his sales team, the better they will be able to service their customers. As such, they will buy more, making the whole team more successful, which is what the boss wanted in the first place.

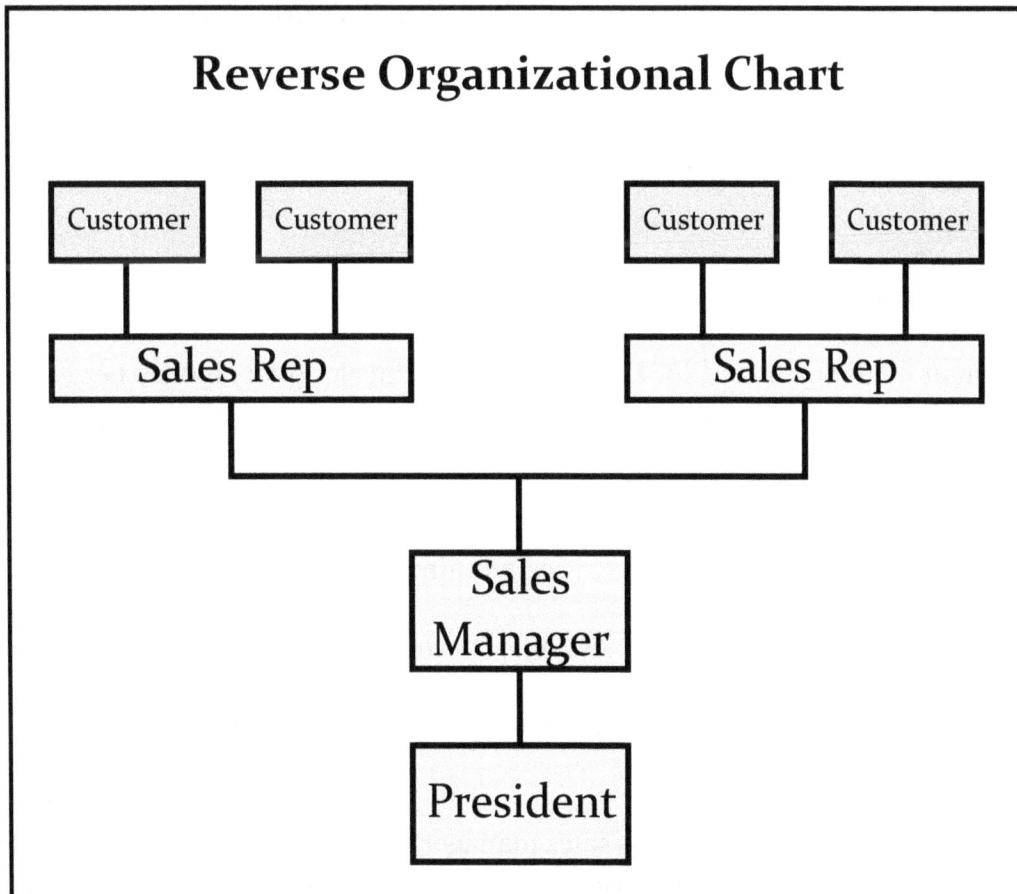

Reverse Organizational Chart

```
[Customer] [Customer]          [Customer] [Customer]
     |         |                    |          |
   [   Sales Rep   ]            [   Sales Rep   ]
          |_____|
                      |
                [   Sales
                   Manager   ]
                      |
                [ President ]
```

Have a mindset that you report to your sales team, as opposed to them reporting to you! Ask them what three things you can do to help them service their customers better. If you make their life easier and keep them happy, they will do a better job. When they do a better job, they will make you look all that much better in your boss's eyes.

Think of all those that report to you as your customer. This is what the best sales managers do. Help you customers get to where they want to go, and they will make you more successful.

The Sales Manager's Job Description

The role of a sales manager can be broken down into four main job functions, all of which are intertwined. If a manager is lacking skills or proper tools in one particular function, all other areas will suffer, and the organization underperforms. However, when all four functions are performed properly, the team excels, and the company flourishes.

Think of each of the four functions as legs of a table. The table is at its sturdiest and most useful when all four legs are the same length. If one leg is shorter, however, the table will lean. It may still function somewhat as a table, but it will not be as useful as a table with all of its legs the same length. If one of legs is missing all together, it may teeter for a short period of time, but eventually, it will just fall over. The same is true for a sales manager who lacks skills in one of the four main job functions.

B2B Sales Skills

Scotty Bowman holds the record for the most wins in the National Hockey League, however due to injury, never played professional hockey himself. Lou Holtz is one of the most successful college football coaches of all time, but he only played two seasons before an injury ended his career. Both coaches achieved great success, not only because they possessed the necessary skills to succeed in their sports, but also because of their ability to teach those skills to others, therefore creating winning teams.

In much the same way a coach of a professional sports team must know how to play the game he coaches, a sales manager must know how to sell the product he represents. Neither has to be a superstar, but both must know enough so that they can teach others how to be successful.

To be a successful business to business sales manager, one must be able to show how, not do for. With this in mind, the first section of this training course will cover the basics of the B2B sales process from a sales manager's perspective. If you need more information on B2B sales from a representative's point of view, please refer to our training course *Action Plan For Sales Success*. Once the basics of business to business sales are understood, a turnkey sales process that can be taught to others must be created.

Recruiting & Hiring

Recruiting and hiring the right sales team is critical for a sales manager's success. The right hires can make the company grow exponentially. The wrong hires, however, are costly!

Studies have shown that hiring the wrong sales person will cost an organization between 3 and 5 times their annual compensation plan in lost revenue, management time, training costs, customer goodwill and expenses. This is a function within the sales manager's job description where you simply cannot afford to make a mistake!

However, a successful sales recruiting program is more than just placing an ad and pouring over hundreds of resumes! In fact, a successful recruiting program requires many tasks. Specifically, a sales manager must:

- Create a detailed description of the available sales position
- Define the ideal candidate for the position
- Design a compensation plan
- Attract the right sales talent to apply for the available position
- Pre-screen the applicants using various methods to ensure a good fit
- Offer the appropriate candidate the position using the right tools

The goal of your recruiting and hiring program is to create a system that increases your chances of making the right choice. The resume doesn't drive sales, the sales person does!

Sales Rep Success Plan Design

The third function of a sales manager's job description is to create a Sales Rep Success Plan. This plan must be detailed, specific, and customized to the product or service that you sell, and for the operating procedures of your company. It should also cover a specified time frame, normally 90 days starting from the new hire's first day of work.

Specifically, your Sales Rep Success Plan should include the following:

- Company Orientation
- Human Resources Procedures
- Compensation Plan Review
- Product Training Schedule
- Sales Training Schedule
- Customer Relationship Management (CRM) System Training
- Order Processing Training
- Company Procedure Training
- Performance Expectations and Monitoring

Your Sales Rep Success Plan is essentially a detailed road map to success for your entire sales team to follow. The more detailed the road map, the greater the chances for success. Remember, no sales manager plans to fail, some just fail to plan!

Ongoing Sales Management

Hiring the right candidates is one thing, keeping them is quite another! Just like Scottie Bowman and Lou Holtz, you are the coach of the team! You must teach what needs to be taught, you must lead where they need to be led, and you must motivate so they follow you there.

Properly managing your team is critical to ensure they produce results today and in the future. To accomplish this, there are many ongoing management tools used by successful managers. They include:

- Group sales meetings
- One on one meetings
- Joint field work
- Testing
- Activity reporting and forecasting tools
- Performance reviews
- Sales incentive contests

When used correctly, ongoing sales management tools can take a sales team to heights only limited by their own imaginations.

Sometimes however, even when the sales manager does everything right, the organization and sales professional must part ways. This could be the employee's choice, or this could be the employer's choice. Therefore, ongoing management techniques must also include an exit strategy, including methods how and when to sever the relationship properly.

In order to be successful in the long term, a sales manager must manage his or her team to create a win-win between the employer and employee. In other words, the organization must be achieving its goals, and so must the sales professional.

B2B SALES DEFINED

Business to business or B2B sales is simply defined as the process where one company exchanges a product or service with another company. Common examples include business equipment, accounting services, and office supplies. The alternative is B2C sales where a company deals directly with the consumers.

Often, the goods being exchanged can be considered both B2B and B2C, however they normally are sold using very different sales processes. For example, companies and consumers both purchase office supplies such as pens and pencils however, a consumer normally buys the products by visiting a retail outlet, whereas a B2B sale tends to be made with the assistance of a sales representative.

When selling in a B2B environment, it is important to remember that business to business sales are different from B2C sales in the following ways:

- B2B buyers are buying for their company, not their households.
- B2B buyers are spending the company's money, not their own.
- More people are involved in a B2B buying decision than a B2C buying decision.
- The sales processes are different.
- There are more B2C prospects than there are business prospects

The B2B Sales Process

Although your sales process may be specific to your industry, every sales process contains three basic steps: prospecting, fact finding, and the presentation of offer stage. Each step leads to the next, where the end result is the sale!

In some transactional sales, the entire sales process may be accomplished in a single call, however many products and services require multiple contacts with the customer.

Prospecting

The first step in any sale is the prospecting call. This includes any type of customer contact that attempts to open the sales process. It could include a telemarketing call, a face to face prospecting call, or a follow up call from previous sales contact. It could also include contact as a result of the prospective customer contacting you first, perhaps via your website or the telephone directory. Sometimes, a sales person may even have to do a combination of different kinds of prospecting calls with the same company.

Essentially, any attempt to initiate the sales process is considered a prospecting call. A prospecting call is considered a success if your sales person and the prospective customer agree to proceed to the next step in the sales process.

Managing the prospecting process is more than telling a sales representative, "Here are your business cards, now go bang on some doors!" To be effective as a sales manager, you must lead your team in the direction where they will be most successful. In other words, which doors should they knock on where they are most likely to make a sale.

It is wrong to believe that every company can and will buy your product or service. For example, it is unlikely that your team will sell restaurant equipment to retail clothing stores. Therefore you need to clearly define the types of companies where your team will most likely find prospects that will buy. Specifically, this definition is commonly referred to as your target market.

A target market definition is a description of your current and future customers. It essentially tells your team what types of companies to prospect. Specifically, your definition should include:

- The type of business or industries in which they operate
- The size of the companies based on the number of employees and/or annual revenue
- The products or services they currently use or are most likely to purchase
- Quantity and frequency of using and reordering your product or service
- Competitive suppliers that they have purchased from or may purchase from in the future
- Related products they may use in addition to your product or service
- Any other common traits that you can identify

Just as it is wrong to believe that every company can and will buy from you, it is also a mistake to believe that every company in your target market can buy from you at any time. For example, it is unlikely that you would lease a new car today when your current lease still has two more years of payments owing. Therefore, to ensure that your team is in the right place at the right time, you must define the time frame when prospects can buy.

To do this, you must know how often a company buys or re-orders your product. Is it weekly, monthly, or even once every five years or more? This is not how often the company uses the product, but how often they renegotiate the contact for the use of your product.

Knowing a company's buying cycle will allow your sales people to determine the timing of the sales opportunity. You can then teach them to prescreen companies in your target market as they prospect. If a company is not a prospect *today*, you can also train them how to determine when they will be. More importantly, you can then structure the sales representative's Follow-Up File or Customer Relationship Management (CRM) System to ensure that your team is always in the right place at the right time.

Lastly, once your team knows where to be, and when to be there, you must train them how to best make contact! Specifically, an effective prospecting approach should be scripted, and should include the following:

- An opening greeting that identifies the key contact
- A headline that generates interest
- Qualifying questions to determine if and when the company is really a prospect
- A statement to obtain agreement to move to the next step

As a sales manager, maximizing sales results includes managing the prospecting stage of the sales process. In a nutshell, you must point your team to the right door, teach them when is the best time to be there, and then coach them on the best method to open it!

For more information on prospecting, please refer to Section 2 of the training course *Action Plan For Sales Success*. It includes many automated tools and describes in detail how to create and track your target market definition, how to create and administer your team's CRM system, and how to properly script your team's prospecting approach to maximize success.

Fact Finding

The second step in the sales process is the fact find, or information gathering stage. At this stage, your team is gathering all the relevant information needed to prepare their offer to the customer. They are identifying the relevant contacts and buying processes within the prospect's organization. They are also determining if sales opportunities actually exist, and if so, what are the time frames of those identified sales opportunities. Again, depending on your industry, a thorough needs analysis may require your sales people to complete more than one fact find appointment within the same company.

Simply put, any sales call that is intended to gather or confirm information about a prospective customer is considered a fact find. A fact find is considered successful if the sales representative and their prospect confirm that the sales process should continue to the last step of the sales process.

One of the most valuable lessons that you can teach your sales team is that prospects buy for their own reasons. Everyone that is involved in a purchasing decision is always thinking "What is in it for me?"

The ultimate objective of any business is to make a profit. The only way for a company to reach this goal is to generate more revenue than it spends on expenses. Therefore any product or service you are selling must be perceived as helping your customer to make a profit, either by increasing revenue of by reducing expenses.

You may be thinking that your products are too insignificant to affect a company's bottom line, but that is not the case. Absolutely everything a company buys affects its bottom line. Even a pencil that lasts longer, or is less expensive than the previous one purchased helps a company to make more profit.

Although businesses buy for profit, the people that work for those businesses buy for their own personal reasons. To complicate matters, sometimes several people are involved in the same corporate purchasing decision, each with their own personal needs and biases. Sometimes these needs can be aligned with each other, and sometimes they can conflict.

Given that everyone's reasons for buying are different, many sales professionals believe that the fact find is the most important stage of the sales process. Not only is this where the prospect tells your sales person what he is going to buy, he is also going to tell them why he is going to buy it!

From a management perspective, when the fact find process is properly planned, everyone wins. Sales professionals who complete a proper fact find have better closing ratios, close higher average sized sales, and sell at a higher average selling price. Customers have higher satisfaction levels because they were involved in the process and as a result, purchased the right product to fill the right need. Lastly, you as a sales manager are happier because you are achieving your goals.

The first key to a successful fact find is to ensure that your team meets with the right people. Normally this is the person in the prospect's organization who has budget accountabilities for the management of your product or service, however, the end user of the product may also be involved.

Depending on your industry, you may have to direct your team to complete more than one fact find. The purpose of the fact find is to discover how, when and why the prospect will buy. Then, and only then, should your sales representative give a price. Train your team not to take short cuts. If in doubt, they should complete another fact find.

The questions asked in a fact find should focus on three main areas:

- General company information
- Customer needs, product and industry specific information
- Financial and buying process information

This is too important a step in the sales process for your sales team to just wing it. The questions themselves should be preplanned and scripted. They should be worded so they create not only a desire to purchase, but also a desire to purchase only from your sales representative!

Everyone wants the cheapest price, but the cheapest price for what they want. They key is *the want*. You must direct your team not to just identify the prospect's needs and wants, but to create them! The most successful sales professionals know that the only way to do that, truly the only way to help the customer buy is to ask the right questions.

Better the fact find, happier the customer, better the paycheque!

For more information on fact finding, please refer to Section 3 of the training course *Action Plan For Sales Success*. It includes automated tools and describes in detail why prospects buy, and how to create and script effective fact finding questions as a result.

Presentation of Offer

The final step in the sales process before completing the sale is the presentation of offer stage. The presentation stage includes any calls that actually present or clarify the offer with the prospect. This could include presenting a written proposal, or an equipment demonstration, or both. It would also include any calls needed to answer any objections the customer may have, or any appointment needed to complete the sales order paperwork.

Any sales call that presents or clarifies what your sales team is selling is considered a presentation. A presentation is successful if your sales representative and their prospect agree to proceed to close the sale by the customer ordering the product.

The exact form of the presentation of offer stage, and the number of calls required to complete it, will depend on your industry and the product or service that you are selling. However, regardless of your industry, the key to an effective presentation is to teach your team to only give their prospect just enough information so that he can make his buying decision. The old saying, "too much information" also applies to sales!

The written proposal is the most common of presentations in business to business sales. This is also where sales representatives make the most mistakes.

For products that are very simple and transactional in nature, it is common to simply write the price on a brochure. A more effective method would be to write the price directly on the contract or sales order form! Not only does this accomplish all of the objectives, but it will also save a lot of time because the sales will close much more quickly.

If a product is larger and more complicated however, some sales representatives believe that their written proposal must be larger and more complicated as well. They believe that the higher the dollar value, the longer the quotation they need to provide. In reality, those pages upon pages of features and specifications actually do more to stall a sale than to move it forward. Most people don't need or want detailed blueprints of framing, plumbing and electrical wiring before they buy their house!

As such, it is highly recommended that your sales team use a standardized proposal template. Not only will it take less time to create a proposal for a prospect, but it will always have just enough of the right information to be effective.

Specifically, the main sections of your team's template should be:

- Title Page
- Company Information
- Present Situation Assessment
- Proposed Solutions
- Financial considerations
- Implementation Schedule & Shared Expectations
- Enclosures

The whole proposal should be no longer than six pages. Shorter is even better, but do not make it longer. Any other detailed information, if needed at all, should be included as an enclosure or an appendix, and not part of the proposal.

Sometimes, depending on your industry, the customer must see, touch or try the product before purchasing. In these situations, it is common for your sales representative to complete a product demonstration. Preparation is critical for a successful demonstration. You must instill in your team that a test drive in a new automobile is not going to be effective unless the sales representative plans ahead and puts gas in the car!

One of the biggest mistakes made by sales representatives in demonstration meetings is that they talk too much, and don't demonstrate enough. Some of the most complicated products can be effectively demonstrated in just 10 minutes! Questions may extend the meeting, but the actual demonstration should be short, to the point, and should be focused on the prospect's needs and benefits. Have your team demonstrate the product to you. If they cannot do so quickly and effectively, then they should practice on you some more before they meet the client.

Demonstrations can sometimes lead to customer requests for on site product trials. The sales representatives, thinking they have done their due diligence, believe that the customer will certainly buy the product once they try it. Whenever possible, regardless if it is commonplace in your industry, do not agree to these trials. The dealership would certainly not allow you to drive a car for a month before buying it, nor would a real estate agent allow you to live in the house before you bought it.

Sometimes, unscrupulous prospects use these trials as a way of getting free use of a machine for an extended period of time, without ever having the intention of actually purchasing. If there are six possible suppliers and each offers one month free trial, the prospect just got a free machine for half a year! Even if this is not the case, the prospect should be able to make a decision without an extended on site trial.

A better strategy for these situations is a limited time conditional order. Conditional orders are a very effective way to ensure that your sales representative is working with a serious buyer. "Yes, Mr. Prospect, you can try this equipment before you purchase. I will post date my sales contract for one week. After that time, if the product has done what we promise it to do, we will execute it. If not, we will tear it up. Does that sound fair?"

If the customer says no to this, chances are he was not ready to buy at the end of the free trial demonstration anyway. However, if the sales process has been followed by your sales representative, including a thorough fact find with a properly fit solution, chances are that the customer will say yes. Then the trial was not merely an on site demonstration for a prospect, it was actually operator training for a customer!

Every sale must have some sort of closing interview before it is complete. This may be a separate meeting, or at the end of a written proposal or demonstration meeting. As a sales manager, you must ensure that your team is always prepared to close a sale. Not only must they know how to handle objections, but they must also know what sales order paperwork is required.

Once the sale is complete, the product is installed, and the customer is realizing the benefits of the solution, your team must have the ability to create a new sales opportunity from the satisfied customer. After all, although the presentation of offer stage can include many different types of presentations, if your team closes one sale and then starts another, you will be very successful.

For more information on the presentation of offer stage of the sales process, please refer to Section 4 of the training course *Action Plan For Sales Success*. It includes automated tools and describes in detail how your team should present your product so that the prospects buy!

WHERE WILL YOU LEAD THE TEAM?

A sales manager must lead the sales team towards achieving a common goal. However in order to lead the team in the right direction, you first define that direction! When you are in a performance-based career like sales, goal setting is vital to your success.

So what are your goals? Is it your company assigned quota? Perhaps. True, your minimum acceptable level of sales performance is important, but it is YOUR goal? Is your quota important enough for you to hold it dear to your heart and make it a driving force in your life? Probably not.

What you do for a living is a means to an end to achieve what you want in life. In other words, the career you have chosen is the way in which you earn income to fund the lifestyle that you want to live. That lifestyle is a personal decision, however determining the income required to fund it is your first step in goal setting.

Before going any further, you need to be able to answer the following question: What is the total annual income you wish to earn to fund your desired lifestyle?

For those who completed the training course *Action Plan For Sales Success,* the spreadsheet *Personal Goal Definition Worksheet.xls* will look familiar, however because goal setting is critical to your success, it must be revisited. The worksheet will help you determine your goals, and the income required to fund it. As you can see from the worksheet, goal setting covers many lifestyle areas and it truly personal in nature. Remember, by signing the form, you are committing to yourself, not anyone else, that you will work towards what you want in life.

One thing that makes sales management unique is that your goals and the goals of each member of your team must align. If they don't, you literally will all be going in different directions. As such, each member of your team should also complete the *Personal Goal Definition Worksheet..*

As the sales manager, you should discuss the *Personal Goal Definition Worksheet* with each member of your team individually. You need know their desired annual incomes so that you can help them develop a plan to earn them. As you achieve your goals by working through your team, you will get where you want to go faster if you help them get to where they want to go!

B2B SALES CONNECTIONS

Personal Goal Definition Worksheet

Enter information in yellow boxes to define your personal goals.

Step 1 - Personal Commitment

I am committed to and will work towards achieving my personal goals as listed below.	
Name	Sam Q. Sales Pro
Date	January 4, 2009 (Today)

Step 2 - Lifestyle & Leisure Time Goals

Next 12 Months	Spend more time with the family; Golf once per week; Make time for my hobby
Next 2 - 4 Years	Buy a house; Buy a car; Take a winter holiday down south; Season's tickets to a local sports team
Long Term	Retire at 55;

Step 3 - Career & Educational Goals

Next 12 Months	Become B2B Sales Connections Accredited; Make quota; Earn the trip to President's Club
Next 2 - 4 Years	Earn a promotion to sales management; Take an adult education course in public speaking
Long Term	Earn a promotion to senior management

Step 4 - Health & Fitness Goals

Next 12 Months	Work out for 30 minutes per day; Quit smoking
Next 2 - 4 Years	Lose 20 pounds
Long Term	Have an annual checkup; Eat healthy food

Step 5 - Spirtual & Community Involvement Goals

Next 12 Months	Volunteer at the hospital; Read 10 minutes per day on self improvement
Next 2 - 4 Years	Join a house of worship
Long Term	Earn Coaching Level 1 Certificate

Step 6 - Financial Goals

Next 12 Months	Get out of credit card debt; Develop a monthly budget
Next 2 - 4 Years	Start an RRSP; Start an TFSA; Invest in the stock market
Long Term	Be mortgage free; Be financially independent

Step 7 - Annual Income Goal

To fund my desired lifestyle and achieve my goals as outlined above, I must earn an annual income of	$	100,000
Signature	*Sam Q. Salespro*	

The Team's Plan of Action

Once you know you total annual income required to fund your desired lifestyle, then you must determine what your sales team needs to accomplish for you to earn that income. Using basic math, you can determine what daily activities your team needs to complete in order for you to achieve your personal goals.

Success in sales is based on the law of averages. Success in sales management is based on managing the activity of the team to those averages.

To determine your team's averages, reverse your sales process. Specifically, you need to calculate how many prospecting calls, fact finds and presentation of offers are required per representative per day to produce the team's sales goal.

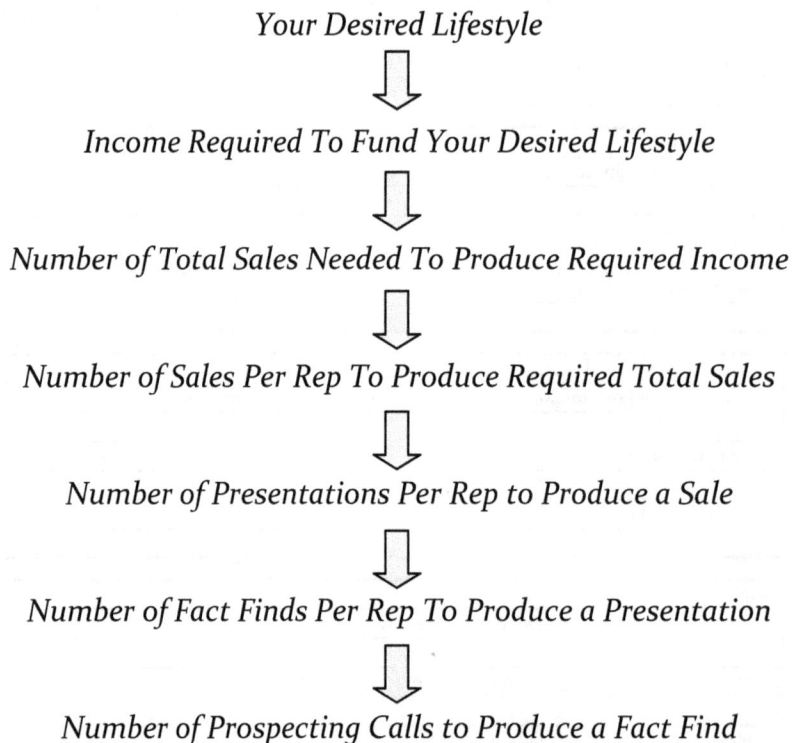

Your Desired Lifestyle

⇩

Income Required To Fund Your Desired Lifestyle

⇩

Number of Total Sales Needed To Produce Required Income

⇩

Number of Sales Per Rep To Produce Required Total Sales

⇩

Number of Presentations Per Rep to Produce a Sale

⇩

Number of Fact Finds Per Rep To Produce a Presentation

⇩

Number of Prospecting Calls to Produce a Fact Find

The spreadsheet *Management Goal Setting & Action Planning Worksheet.xls* is an Excel file that will calculate this automatically for you. It is similar to the sales representative version found in the training course *Action Plan For Sales Success*, however the management version works from a sales team perspective. Enter the data in the yellow boxes and the end result will be what each member of your team must accomplish each day to achieve their goals. An example is shown below.

B SALES CONNECTIONS

Management Goal Setting & Action Planning Worksheet

Enter data in yellow boxes to calculate the daily activities required to achieve your goals.

What is the total annual income you wish to earn to fund your lifestyle?	$ 150,000.00
What is your base salary?	$ 50,000.00
What is your average monthly bonus earned?	$ 500.00
What is your average commission rate?	2.00%
What is your team's average size sale?	$ 10,000.00
How many sales people are on your team?	10.0
How many presentations does it take a sales person to make a sale?	3.0
How many fact finds does it take a sales person to make a presentation?	2.0
How many prospecting calls does it take a sales person to book a fact find?	15.0

SALES TEAM ACTION PLAN

Total Team Annual Sales Volume Required for Goal Attainment	$ 4,700,000.00
Total Team Monthly Sales Volume Required for Goal Attainment	$ 391,666.67
Total Number of Sales Required Per Month	40
Total Number of Sales Required Per Week	10.0
Total Number of Presentations Required Per Month	120
Total Number of Presentations Required Per Week	30.00
Total Number of Fact Finds Required Per Month	240
Total Number of Fact Finds Required Per Week	60.00
Total Number of Prospecting Calls Required Per Month	3,600
Total Number of Prospecting Calls Required Per Week	900
Total Number of Prospecting Calls Required Per Day	180

SALE PERSON ACTION PLAN

Annual Sales Volume Required Per Sales Person	$ 470,000.00
Monthly Sales Volume Required Per Sales Person	$ 39,166.67
Number of Sales Required Per Month Per Sales Person	4.0
Number of Sales Required Per Week Per Sales Person	1
Number of Presentations Required Per Month Per Sales Person	12
Number of Presentations Required Per Week Per Sales Person	3
Number of Fact Finds Required Per Month Per Sales Person	24
Number of Fact Finds Required Per Week Per Sales Person	6
Number of Prospecting Calls Required Per Month Per Sales Person	360
Number of Prospecting Calls Required Per Week Per Sales Person	90
Number of Prospecting Calls Required Per Day Per Sales Person	18

If you are not familiar with Excel, you can determine your team's required daily activities by just filling in the form contained in Appendix A.

Achieving the goal of earning your desired income is made much easier when you know what each representative needs to do each day to contribute to the overall success of the team. Managing them to complete a daily activity is much easier than managing them to achieve an annual target. By breaking out a larger task into the daily activities required to achieve it, you greatly increase your chances of getting to where you want to go.

Managing The Team's Sales Funnel

Sales people do not wait until they close one sale before starting another. In fact, when you assess all the active prospects that your team is working on, there will be many potential sales on the go, all at different stages of the sales process.

A graphical representation of this is called the sales funnel. The team's potential sales are poured into the top of the funnel. As the sales process proceeds, the funnel narrows, until closed sales pour out the bottom.

As a sales manager, you must ensure that the team always has a sufficient number of potential sales entering and completed sales exiting your funnel. By using the sales process averages calculated earlier, you can determine the total number and dollar value of sales that the team needs at each level of the sales funnel to achieve your goals.

The spreadsheet *Sales Funnel Management Worksheet.xls*, first introduced in the training course *Action Plan For Sales Success,* is an Excel workbook that will track your team's sales funnel automatically for

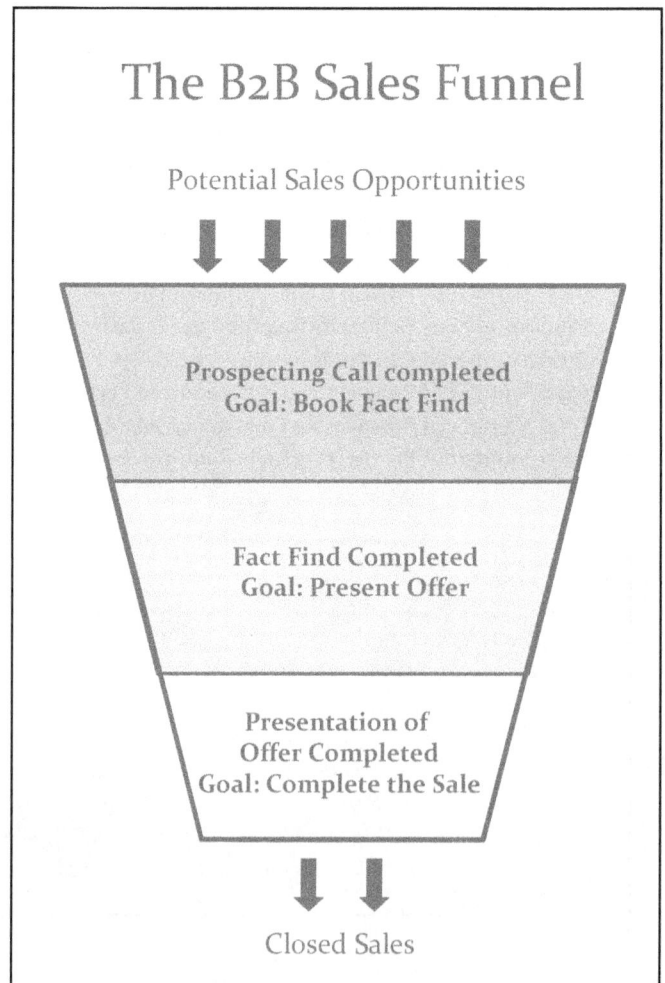

The B2B Sales Funnel

Potential Sales Opportunities

Prospecting Call completed
Goal: Book Fact Find

Fact Find Completed
Goal: Present Offer

Presentation of
Offer Completed
Goal: Complete the Sale

Closed Sales

you.   First, enter all of the team's prospects in the yellow boxes on the worksheet "Sales Funnel Prospects". There are only three options that can be entered for the sales process step completed: Fact Find, Presentation and Sales completed. If you click in a box in this column, a drop down menu will appear so that you can just select one of the three choices.

B B SALES *CONNECTIONS*

Sales Funnel Prospects

Enter data in yellow boxes each week to calculate your sales process averages. At the end of each month, delete all completed sales.

Company	Last Step of the Sales Process Completed?	Value of Potential Sale
ABC Company	Fact Find	$ 24,942.00
Profit Inc.	Presentation	$ 5,235.00
Super Sales Rep Corp.	Sale Completed	$ 7,565.00

As you enter your prospects, the spreadsheet will calculate the dollar value of all the prospects in each step of the sales process. The results will appear in the worksheet "Funnel Management Worksheet". This worksheet also creates your target sales funnel based on your sales process averages.

B B SALES *CONNECTIONS*

Sales Funnel Management Worksheet

Enter data in yellow boxes each week to calculate your sales process averages.

Your Monthly Sales Objective	$ 45,833.00
The number of presentations it takes you to make a sale	3.00
The number of fact finds it takes you to make a presentation	2.00

Sales Funnel Targets	Sales Process Step	Sales Funnel Actuals
$ 274,998.00	Fact Finds Completed	$ 302,945.00
$ 137,499.00	Presentations Completed	$ 153,940.00
$ 45,833.00	Sales Completed	$ 52,000.00

By comparing the target sales funnel to your actual sales funnel, you can see if the team is on target to reach its goals. Using your averages, you can actually forecast the team's future sales over a given time frame.

The example above shows a healthy sales funnel. There are sufficient prospects at each level of the sales process to support the next stage, and the end result should be the attainment of your monthly sales objective.

However, perhaps the worksheet shows that you do not have enough prospects at the presentation stage to achieve your monthly sales target. You would therefore need to move more of your potential sales from the fact find stage to the presentation stage as soon as possible. Or perhaps the worksheet shows that you do not have enough customers at the fact find stage. You would therefore need to add more prospects into the top of your sales funnel immediately to ensure that you stay on track.

Knowledge is power. Knowing exactly where the team stands, and more importantly if you need to make changes to get them back on course, is more than half the battle in getting to where you want to go.

CONCLUSION

The sales force drives the company's revenue and it the sales manager's job to drive the sales force. If a sales manager does not perform, the company does not survive, let alone prosper! It is no wonder that many consider the function of sales management to be the most important within a company.

To be successful as a sales manager, you must teach the team what needs to be taught, you must lead where they need to be led, and you must motivate so they follow you there. To do this effectively, you must help your customer, namely your sales team, get what they want, and not just focus on what you want.

"Give a man a fish and you feed him for a day. Teach a man to fish and you feed him for a lifetime." – Chinese Proverb

APPENDIX – MANUAL CALCULATION FORMS

For those of you who are not familiar with Excel spreadsheets, all the calculations discussed in this training module can also be done manually. Simply print the forms on the following pages and follow the instructions.

Excel is a very common business software program. It is highly recommended that you take the time to learn the basics. Not only will you find that it can make your life much easier, you will find it to be a very profitable business tool as well.

Personal Goal Definition
Worksheet

Step 1 - Personal Commitment	
I am committed to and will work towards achieving my personal goals as listed below.	
Name	
Date	

Step 2 - Lifestyle & Leisure Time Goals	
Next 12 Months	
Next 2 - 4 Years	
Long Term	

Step 3 - Career & Educational Goals	
Next 12 Months	
Next 2 - 4 Years	
Long Term	

Step 4 - Health & Fitness Goals	
Next 12 Months	
Next 2 - 4 Years	
Long Term	

Step 5 - Spirtual & Community Involvement Goals	
Next 12 Months	
Next 2 - 4 Years	
Long Term	

Step 6 - Financial Goals	
Next 12 Months	
Next 2 - 4 Years	
Long Term	

Step 7 - Annual Income Goal	
To fund my desired lifestyle and achieve my goals as outlined above, I must earn an annual income of	
Signature	

Management Goal Setting & Action Planning Worksheet

SALES TEAM ACTION PLAN

1. What is the total annual income you wish to earn to fund your lifestyle?

2. What is your base salary?

3. What is your average monthly bonus earned?

4. Amount of commission income required to reach annual income goal. (#1-(#2 + #3))

5. What is your average commission rate?

6. Total annual sales volume required. ((#4 / #5) x 100)

7. Monthly sales volume required. (#6 / 12)

8. What is your team's average size of sale?

9. Total number of sales required per month. (#7 / #8)

10. Total number of sales required per week. (#9 / 4)

11. How many presentations does it take your team to make a sale?

12. Total Number of presentations required per month. (#9 x #11)

13. Total Number of presentations required per week. (#12 / 4)

14. How many fact finds does it take your team to make a presentation?

15. Total Number of fact finds required per month. (#13 x #14)

16. Total Number of fact finds required per week. (#15 / 4)

17. How many prospecting calls does it take your to book a fact find?

18. Total Number of prospecting calls required per month. (#15 x #17)

19. Total Number of prospecting calls required per week. (#18 / 4)

20. Total Number of prospecting calls required per day. (#19 / 5)

SALE PERSON ACTION PLAN

21. How many sales People On Your Team

22. Annual Sales Volume Required Per Sales Person (#6 / #21)

23. Monthly Sales Volume Required Per Sales Person (#7 / #21)

24. Number of Sales Required Per Month Per Sales Person (#9 / #21)

25. Number of Sales Required Per Week Per Sales Person (#10 / #21)

26. Number of Presentations Required Per Month Per Sales Person (#12 / #21)

27. Number of Presentations Required Per Week Per Sales Person (#13 / #21)

28. Number of Fact Finds Required Per Month Per Sales Person (#15 / #21)

29. Number of Fact Finds Required Per Week Per Sales Person (#16 / #21)

30. Number of Prospecting Calls Required Per Month Per Sales Person (#18 / #21)

31. Number of Prospecting Calls Required Per Week Per Sales Person (#19 / #21)

32. Number of Prospecting Calls Required Per Day Per Sales Person (#20 / #21)

Sales Funnel Management Worksheet

Your Monthly Sales Objective	
The number of presentations it takes you to make a sale	
The number of fact finds it takes you to make a presentation	

Sales Funnel Targets	Sales Process Step	Sales Funnel Actuals
$ - (Your Monthly Value for Presentations Below X The Number of Fact Finds to Make a Presentation)	Fact Finds Completed	$ - (The Total of Fact Finds Completed from Sales Funnel Prospects Form)
$ - (Your Monthly Sales Objective X The Number of Presentations to Make a Sale)	Presentations Completed	$ - (The Total of Presentations Completed from Sales Funnel Prospects Form)
$ - (Your Monthy Sales Objective)	Sales Completed	$ - (The Total of Sales Completed from Sales Funnel Prospects Form)

Chapter 2 – Eagles or Turkeys? Recruiting and Hiring The Right Sales Professional

"It's hard to soar like an eagle
 when you work with turkeys!" –
Author Unknown

A SUCCESSFUL RECRUITING PROGRAM

Recruiting and hiring the right sales team is critical for a sales manager's success. If you make the right choices and hire the perfect fit for your sales organization, the company can grow exponentially. If you make the wrong hiring choices, however, the company loses much more than just the wages that were paid.

Studies have shown that hiring the wrong sales person will cost an organization between 3 and 5 times their annual compensation plan in lost revenue, management time, training costs, customer goodwill and expenses. These losses can be further compounded by the effect a bad hire has on your existing team. This mistake can demoralize a sales team just as a cancer can destroy a healthy body, with poor sales performance as the end result. Recruiting and hiring is a function of the sales manager's job where you simply cannot afford to make a mistake!

A successful sales recruiting program, however, is more than just placing an ad, pouring over hundreds of applications, and then picking the candidate with the best resume. A resume doesn't drive sales, a sales person does! In fact, a successful recruiting program requires many tasks. Specifically, a sales manager must:

- Design a compensation plan to offer to the candidate
- Create a comprehensive job description
- Define the ideal candidate for your organization
- Attract the right sales talent to apply for the available position
- Pre-screen the applicants using various methods to ensure a good fit
- Offer the right candidate the position using the right tools

The goal of your recruiting and hiring program is to find the right fit for both the employer and the employee. To do so, you must create a system that not only maximizes your chances of making the right choice, but also minimizes your chances of making the wrong choice.

Compensation Plan Design

It has been said that in sales, the employer employee relationship is like a marriage, with some being the perfect partnership lasting for years, while others are short term disasters that never should have happened in the first place.

Although the analogy may be a stretch for some, it is certain that the relationship between the sales professional and the sales organization is essentially a financial arrangement. The employer must believe that he is getting good value for the dollars he is paying the employee, and the employee must feel that is he being paid what he is worth. Otherwise the relationship will not last.

The details of this financial arrangement are outlined in the compensation plan. If the analogy holds true and the relationship is like a marriage, then the sales compensation plan is the marriage license that binds them.

Every company pays their sales staff differently. Salaries, bonuses, and commissions, are just a few of the components a sales manager can use to create a compensation plan. Before you decide how you should compensate your sales team, you first must decide how much.

How Much Should You Pay?

The first step in designing your sales compensation plan is to determine how much overall compensation you are going to pay your sales people. Although there is no one right answer to this question, and it may vary greatly from one industry to the next, it is recommended that you compensate your sales representatives 20 percent of gross profit on average. For our purposes, we are going to define gross profit as the selling price less the cost of goods sold.

The actual percentage paid per sales representative can vary anywhere between 15 and 25 percent of gross profit, depending on the person's productivity. Someone who earns more that 25 percent of gross profit is not selling enough to warrant their compensation, whereas a top producer earning less than 15 percent is not being paid fairly. Although this range may seem broad, a compensation plan that pays 20 percent of gross profit when the sales representative is producing at quota is usually considered very acceptable to both the employer and employee.

It is common in many sales organizations to base compensation on gross sales or gross revenues, as opposed to gross profit. The thinking here is that sales people should only be concerned with the sales they produce, as opposed to how much profit the company earns. Although this works very well in organizations where sales people are not allowed to give price discounts, it is very dangerous where they can. In these circumstances, it is possible for sales people to give such big discounts that the company actually loses money when they win the sale! Compensating sales representatives on gross profit avoids this, and ensures the company only pays compensation on profitable sales.

Even though your total amount of sales compensation should be based on gross profit, sometimes it is not desirable to show your gross profit to your sales team. Or perhaps it will be easier for administration purposes to show the overall compensation as a percentage of sales. The *Gross Profit Compensation Conversion Worksheet.xls* is a workbook that converts your gross profit compensation percentage into your percentage of sales.

B B SALES CONNECTIONS

Gross Profit Compensation Conversion Worksheet

Enter data in the yellow boxes to convert the overall amount of sales compensation to a percentage of sales.	
Desired Percentage of Gross Profit for Overall Sale Compensation	20.0%
Product Selling Price	$ 10,000.00
Less Cost of Goods Sold	$ 6,000.00
Gross Profit	$ 4,000.00
Total Desired Sales Compensation	$ 800.00
Desired Sales Compensation Percentage of Sales	8.0%

For example, if you sold your widgets for a total of $10,000, and those same widgets cost you $6,000 to produce, your gross profit is calculated to be $4,000. If your goal is to pay overall sales compensation at 20 percent of gross profit, that equates to 8% of your sales.

If you are not familiar with Excel, determine your desired sales compensation as percentage of sales by dividing the total desired sales compensation by your total sales.

How Should You Pay Compensation?

Now that you have decided how much to pay your sales team, the next step is to decide how to pay it. For sales compensation, this is essentially a decision between how much guaranteed income and how much performance based income to pay your sales team:

- Guaranteed Income – Compensation that is paid regardless of the sales results of the sales representative. Common examples include base salaries and automobile allowances.
- Performance Based Income – Compensation that is paid only when a specified level of performance is achieved. Common examples include commissions, bonuses, profit sharing and incentive contests.

The combinations of guaranteed and performance based income for sales professionals are endless, as are the debates among sales managers as to how the exact mix should be calculated. Some believe if you have too high a guaranteed income, you will not create an environment where your sales people understand that they must sell at a minimum level in order to earn an income. Others believe basing compensation solely on sales performance will create representatives that are too self serving, and customer service will suffer. Those on this side of the debate also believe that performance only based compensation plans can also make it more difficult to find qualified sales people since most are expecting a based plus commission structure.

Before you decide on the type of compensation plan that is right for your organization, you must consider the duties of your sales team. Generally, the more account management and customer service duties required, the higher the percentage of guaranteed income, whereas positions that rely heavily on sales production or new customer acquisitions tend to be more performance based. If you think of this another way, the structure of your compensation plan is to encourage and reward desired behavior. If the desired behavior can be quantified and measured, then it can be compensated with performance based income. Sales dollars produced or new customers acquired can easily be quantified and measured, whereas quantifying good customer service is much more difficult. The more subjective the criteria are, the higher the potential for compensation disputes with management over when a representative should and shouldn't be compensated.

The timing of the products and services that you sell should also be considered when determining the split between guaranteed and performance based income. If sales cycles are long, a commission only compensation plan may result in long periods without any pay. It would be difficult for almost anyone to budget for regular monthly living expenses if they are paid as infrequently as only once per year.

The split between guaranteed and performance based income is also affected by your product and your local labour market conditions. What is the norm for your industry? What are your competitors offering? Are other sales organizations in your area advertising positions with or without base salaries? Simply put, if you want the best sales people, you must be competitive in your marketplace.

Your compensation plan is also affected by the personalities of your sales team. Some sales professionals, although top producers, simply will not work solely on performance based income because they feel that their sales experience has earned them a salary. Others find it too stressful, while some prefer the competitiveness of it.

In the end, the amount of guaranteed income versus performance based income paid doesn't really matter as long as you stay within the average 20 percent of gross profit at target quota. If this is adhered to, you will strike the needed balance between what works for the organization, and what works for the employee.

How To Determine Target Quota?

Like the issue of how much guaranteed versus performance based income to pay, determining a sales professional's target quota is a heavily debated topic among sales managers. On one end of the spectrum is the belief that quotas should be low enough so the entire sales team achieves it. This results in a feeling of accomplishment, creating a more productive environment. On the other end is the belief that quotas should be set so unreachably high that everyone is always striving to attain them.

Having experienced the two programs in both direct sales and sales management roles, it is believed that the right quota level is somewhere in between. You want your quota high enough that your sales people have to push themselves to reach it, but you don't want it so high it is demoralizing because no one can. Quotas need to be challenging, but achievable. After all, wouldn't having your entire team selling at quota be a nice problem to have as sales manager?

As quotas work best when they are challenging yet achievable, it stands to reason that as time goes by, your target quotas will need to be adjusted. As sales representatives stretch to make this year's quota, it may not be challenging for them to reach the same sales level next year. The key when adjusting quotas is not to make changes too frequently, and not to make the changes too drastic. A reasonable percentage increase annually is much more effective than an unrealistic doubling of quotas every quarter.

To set your target quotas, first look at your existing team. What is the average among all of your sales representatives? How many members of your team are above average? At what level are your top producers selling? As a general rule, if 25 percent of your team is at quota or above, your assigned quotas are in the right ball park. If no one is reaching quota, they are simply too high. On the reverse, if everyone is above quota, although this would be a nice problem to have, chances are that your quota is too low.

A more scientific approach to setting target quotas is to analyze the costs of running your business. If you know how much each sales representative must produce to cover your fixed costs and provide you with a reasonable amount of profit, you can determine your target quota.

The *Target Quota Calculation Worksheet.xls* shown on the next page is a workbook that will help you determine the target quota for your sales team. It is a powerful yet easy to use tool that will allow you to quickly and accurately determine the quotas you need based on your unique requirements. As you enter data into the yellow boxes, the spreadsheet will automatically calculate your breakeven sales level, as well as your target quota for each sales representative.

As you can see from the worksheet, your target quota for your sales force is affected by many variables. If your profit objective or the size of your sales team changes, so should your target quotas. Fixed costs like rent and administration which must be paid even if your team does not sell anything must also be considered, in addition to your gross margins. Knowing that each member of your sales team will probably not reach quota, you may want to build in a buffer before finalizing your targets. Lastly, ensuring that your sales representatives income goals are in line with their target quota attainment will ensure that they are motivated to reach them.

Finally to ensure that your target quotas are achievable, divide the total target quota by your average size sale. This calculates the total number of sales required to reach target quota. If the most your best sales representative ever produced was five sales in a month, but your quota requires all of your representatives to now sell ten, then some adjustments will need to be made. On the other hand, if the results are reversed, then it will be that much easier for you to demonstrate to your team that quotas are attainable. Remember, once your team believes that they can reach their goals, they are half way to making them happen!

B B SALES CONNECTIONS

Target Quota Calculation Worksheet

Enter data in the yellow boxes to calculate the annual target quota per sales representative.

Desired Percentage of Gross Profit for Overall Sales Compensation	20.0%
Desired Total Annual Net Profit	$ 400,000
Total Annual Fixed Costs	$ 1,000,000
Total Number of Sales Representatives on Sales Team	5
Product Selling Price	$ 10,000
Less Cost of Goods Sold	$ 6,000
Gross Profit	$ 4,000
Less Sales Compensation	$ 800
Less Other Variable Costs	$ -
Contribution to Fixed Costs	$ 3,200
Gross Profit Margin	40.0%
Contribution To Fixed Costs Margin	32.0%
Total Sales Required To Break Even	$ 3,125,000
Total Sales Required Per Sales Representative Break Even	$ 625,000
Total Sales Required To Reach Profit Targets	$ 4,375,000
Total Sales Per Representative Required To Reach Profit Targets	$ 875,000
Quota Buffer Percentage	25%
Calculated Annual Quota Per Representative With Buffer	$ 1,093,750
Estimated Total Annual Compensation At Target Quota Per Sales Representative	$ 87,500
Desired Income Of Sales Representative	$ 100,000
Sales Required for Sales Representative to Earn Desired Income Per Year	$ 1,250,000
Percentage of Quota Required To Earn Desired Income	114.3%

Other Compensation Plan Design Considerations

It is safe to say that there are as many sales compensation plans as there are sales organizations.   In fact, you would be hard pressed to find two identical sales compensation plans across different companies.

Sales compensation design is such an important yet debated topic that there have been volumes written on this subject alone!   The bottom line is that there are no absolutes, what works in one situation is not guaranteed to work in another.

When designing your plan, you really are only limited by your own imagination. Although there are no right and wrong ways, experience has shown that you should keep the following in mind when creating your compensation plan:

- Compensation plans work best if they are easily understood and simple to administer. If a sales representative cannot quickly and simply calculate what he would be paid on any given sale, chances are the plan is too complicated.

- Compensation plans that have a declining commission rate as sales volumes increase, or plans that are capped with a maximum payout are not recommended in any circumstances. This is basically a disincentive to over achieve! If there is less money to be made on the last sale this month versus the first sale next month, chances are that the order will be delayed.

- Plans that have escalating scales of performance based compensation are more effective. Every sale that is submitted once your fixed costs are paid is pure profit. In the example above, once a sales representative sells over $625,000, he has reached his breakeven point and is only now making money for the company. The sooner this point is reached, the better! To motivate the representative to reach this point as fast as possible, place a higher portion of available performance based income on all sales above $625,000 or whatever quota you determine as your break even point.

- Payment of the performance based elements should only be made upon the product delivery, customer acceptance sign off, or invoice payment. This ensures the sales professional stays engaged with the customer throughout the entire process. History shows that sales orders that pay commissions where the sales representative has only submitted the contract are more likely to be cancelled. After all, it takes just as much administration time and effort to take a sale off the books, than it is to enter it, not to mention the animosity it creates with the sales representative when you have to charge back the commission.

- Sales perks and contests can work very well as part of your overall compensation plan design, depending on the time frame of the contest. If a sales contest is run for the entire year, its cost should be included in your overall sales compensation as 20 percent of gross profit calculation, but if the time frame is shorter, it should not. The design of sales contests and their use as ongoing sales management tools will be discussed elsewhere in this training course, however at this point it is worth noting that there is no prize too outrageous or too expensive to offer. Whatever the cost, simply adjust the target quota required to earn it.

What Are Your Expectations?

Do you need a part time inside sales representative, a full time outside sales person or an independent sales agent? Do you need them to focus on new customer acquisitions, or on account management? What is the annual sales quota and how much travel will be required to reach it? Will the sales person work from home, or will they need to report to your office each day? Should they have experience working for your competition, or do you prefer candidates who are new to your industry?

Before you can hire your ideal sales professional, you first must define what job you need them to do. This should include an outline of the specific requirements and accountabilities of the available sales position.

By completing the *Job Description Form* shown below, you will create an outline of what you expect from this sales role within your organization. Once that is complete, then you can start to think about the ideal candidate for the position.

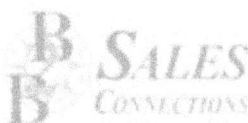

JOB DESCRIPTION FORM

Division/Department: _____ Sales Department _____

Position Title: _____ Account Manager _____

Position Reporting To: _____ Regional Sales Manager _____

Position Type: _____ Outside Sales _____

Location Where Position Will Be Based: _____ Toronto Branch Office _____

Geographic Description of Territory Assignment: _____ Western Toronto _____

Travel Requirements: _____ District – travel within an easy drive; no overnight stays

General Job Description: _____ To sell widgets and gadgets to new and existing customers within the assigned territory. To service those clients to ensure that an ongoing customer relationship is maintained. _____

Work Experience Requirements: _____ 3 to 5 years of previous B2B sales experience __

Education Requirements: _____ College or University Degree _____

Other Requirements: _____ Basic Computer Skills, including Word, Excel, & Email; Bilingual in English and French Preferred _____

Annual Sales Quota: _____ $750,000 _____

Other Performance Targets: _____ 2 New Customers/Month; 95% Price Performance __

Percentage of Time to Be Spent on New Customer Acquisition: _____ 50% _____

Target Income at Quota: _____ $100,000/year **Base Salary:** _____ $40,000/year _____

Other Compensation Included: _____ Automobile Allowance; Cell Phone Allowance; Group Benefits; 3 Weeks Paid Vacation _____

Who Is Your Ideal Candidate?

Now that you have defined what needs to be done, you must define the ideal person to do it. But who is the ideal sales professional? What does the perfect candidate look like? What do they sound like? What makes them tick?

If you asked a room full of successful sales managers to make a list of the common personality traits of their ideal sales candidate, you would probably be surprised at how many different the answers were. There would certainly be common attributes on each list, but overall there would not be two answers exactly the same.

Every company is different and every product is different. Therefore every sales manager's ideal sales candidate will be different. One of the biggest myths in sales is that "one size fits all". There is no one definition of the ideal sales candidate that fits everyone, but there is a one definition of the ideal sales candidate that fits you.

To create a profile of your ideal candidate, you should begin by looking at you existing sales team. Think for a moment of your top sales person. If you could wave a magic wand and fill your entire sales team with clones of your top representative, would you? Of course you would! Can you think of a better way to guarantee that you make the perfect hire than by cloning someone whom you know can already do the job?

Actually, cloning your top representatives is not as far fetched as it might seem. You just first have to define what it is you are looking for. One option to help you accomplish this is to use sales aptitude testing. These assessments and analysis tools require only a few minutes to complete, and are very inexpensive, yet the value of the information they give is immeasurable. Once you know what personality traits and skills your top representatives possess, you can look for the same attributes when assessing new candidates.   In other words, legalized cloning!

Another option to identify the personality traits of your top performers is to use the *Ideal Sales Candidate Definition Worksheet* on the next page. First enter in the names of your best five sales professionals. They may be on your team now, or they may have worked for you in the past. Listed in alphabetical order in the left hand column are the most common personality traits of successful sales professionals. Select the top five to ten traits that could be used to describe each sales professional, and put a "Y" in the appropriate box. The traits with the highest total in the "Ideal Sales Candidate" column would then create your profile of your ideal sales professional.

Ideal Sales Candidate Definition Worksheet

B B SALES CONNECTIONS

Enter the names of your top 4 sales professionals in the space provided. Then select their top personality traits that despcribe them by putting a "Y" in the appropriate box.

Name of Sales Professional #1:	Sam Sales
Name of Sales Professional #2:	Pat Prospector
Name of Sales Professional #3:	Fred Factfinder
Name of Sales Professional #4:	Percy Presenter
Name of Sales Professional #5:	Colleen Closer

Common Sales Personality Trait	Sam Sales	Pat Prospector	Fred Factfinder	Percy Presenter	Colleen Closer	Ideal Sales Candidate
	Y	Y	Y	Y	Y	
Action Oriented						
Ambitious	Y				Y	2
Analytical						
Assertive						
Coachable		Y	Y			2
Competitive	Y	Y	Y	Y		4
Composed						
Creative						
Curious						
Diciplined	Y	Y	Y			3
Direct						
Driven						
Empathetic						
Energetic						
Enthusiatic						
Entrepreneurial						
Ethical						
Focused				Y		1
Good Listener					Y	1
Grounded						
Hard Working						
Honest						
Independent						
Money Motivated			Y		Y	2
Open Minded						
Optimistic						
Organized	Y			Y	Y	3
Outgoing						
Persistant		Y		Y	Y	3
Personable						
Persuasive						
Results Oriented						
Self Confident						
Self Motivated	Y	Y	Y	Y		4
Tough Minded						

Your final Ideal Sales Candidate Profile should not include every trait that appears on the worksheet, only the top five. If the results do not produce a clear profile, then you could give more weight to the results of only certain sales professionals or specific characteristics. For example, perhaps you would give a higher rating to your top two sales representatives, as opposed to your top five. The goal is to create a definitive candidate profile, but not with a description so broad that every applicant would fit within it.

This worksheet can still be used if you do not have an existing sales team to assess. This could be the case if you are building your sales team from the ground up. It is common for people with similar personalities to work well together. Therefore, assuming you have been successful in sales in the past, you could assess yourself. You could also ask people you have worked with previously to describe the dominate personality traits that have made you successful. Having multiple assessments of the same individual can be very effective in creating an ideal candidate profile.

If you do not have sales experience, and you do not know any other sales professional that you could assess on the *Ideal Sales Candidate Definition Worksheet*, you can still create your profile by referring back to your job description created earlier. Although much harder to do, it is possible if you keep in mind the following general rules of thumb:

- If you are looking for a sales person who will focus on account management then your ideal candidate will need relationship building skills. Common personality traits to include in your profile would be empathetic, a good listener, outgoing, and personable.
- If you need a hunter sales person who will focus on finding new customers then you need someone who is persistent, competitive, tough minded, and assertive.
- If you want to pay a performance based income you will need someone who is self-motivated. Common personality traits to include would be money motivated, driven, entrepreneurial, and hard working.
- If you have a high priced product or service with long complicated buying cycles and higher sales quotas, then you will need to look for someone who is more analytical, creative, open minded and composed.
- The more travel required, the more independent your ideal candidate will need to be. They will also need to be organized and disciplined.

There is no one right answer and each personality trait can exist in each candidate in varying degrees. The key is you need to have a picture in your mind of what you are looking for in a candidate so that you will recognize it when you see it.

Attracting Talent

Now that you have defined the job you have available, the compensation plan you are willing to pay, and the ideal sales professional you want to fill the position, the next step is to attract the right sales candidates to apply for it.

It is common knowledge that recruiting qualified sales professionals is not an easy task. Study after study states that finding the right sales talent is one of the biggest concerns facing sales organizations. In fact, many managers would agree that this is the number one staffing challenge they face, and that sales jobs are the most difficult positions to fill.

Since it is extremely unlikely that you have qualified potential sales candidates banging down your front door begging to work for you, you are going to have to advertise. However, in today's world, a successful sales recruiting program is more than just placing an ad in your local newspaper and pouring over hundreds of resumes! You have to put your line in the water where the fish are!

Where To Advertise

Where are today's job seekers searching for their next career opportunity? Most are turning online. According to Media Metrix, the internet is the first and often the only research tool that candidates use for their career search. Northstar Research Partners reported in 2008 that more than 60 percent of Canadians believe they will find their next job online. Since technology is only going to become a bigger part of our lives in the future, this statistic will certainly continue to rise. This is further evidenced in the sharp decline in the number of advertisements and circulation of newspapers as compared to just a few years ago. In many cases, placing an advertisement in the newspaper to find sales people is a bad investment decision. Just ask a few of your targeted candidates how many even looked at the paper as part of a job search strategy.

The question is not whether you need to advertise your available sales positions on the internet, the question is where! The answer is simply where your ideal sales candidates are most likely to see it. Narrowcasting on specialized industry or sales job boards is far more effective that broadcasting on overcrowded, multiple career websites.

When you advertise on these mega job boards, you really have no idea how many qualified candidates will view it. It is far too easy for your posting to get lost in the clutter with hundreds, if not thousands, of competitive and non career related ads. This lack of target marketing is not acceptable in your marketing advertising campaigns, nor should it be in your recruiting advertising campaigns.

Taking this a step further, even specialized sales job websites might not provide the proper focus you need. If you are in B2B sales, why spend your money on a job posting that gets mixed in with hundreds of B2C, retail and multi-level marketing sales positions. Specialized business to business sales sites attract B2B sales professionals, and that means better qualified sales professionals will view your ad. The more that view it, the more that will apply.

One option to using job boards that charge you to post your available positions is to advertise on the free internet classified and job board websites. The reality is that you get what you pay for. First of all, you will receive an incredible amount of unwanted email. There are many stories of reply email addresses that needed to be shut down shortly after the advertisement was placed because the email servers were inundated with spam, junk resumes and unqualified candidates applying from all around the world. The problem is the good is mixed in with the bad, and it is like looking for a needle in a haystack to find it. By the time you sort through all the unwanted junk responses, the fact is that you will have very few, if any, qualified applicants to show for all the time you invested.

There is an old saying that states, "if it sounds too good to be true, it usually is!" Most often, advertising for free sounds too good to be true. In the end, it is usually cheaper and faster to pay for your recruiting advertising on a specialized job board than it is to advertise on a "free" website.

Lastly, ensure that you advertise your available positions in the Career Section of your own website. It will only be seen if someone was already going to your website for another reason, but why waste the chance to attract them as a sales candidate once they are there.

Just placing your advertisement in the right place will not guarantee the desired response. Remember that sales positions are considered the hardest positions to fill. Your ad will be competing against other ads placed by sales organizations that are also looking for the perfect sales candidates.

You must write your ad so that you will attract the right sales talent to apply. Create a headline that will catch their attention and make them want to read it. Write the copy so that you answer the question "what's in it for me?" from the applicant's perspective, not yours. Briefly outline your requirements and expectations. Save the long and boring company history that you see in most employment ads for your annual report.
Shown below is an example of an effective business to business sales employment ad. Once customized for your situation, and posted in the right place so that it is targeted directly to business to business sales professionals, it is sure to attract the right candidates to apply to your available position.

Do You Want To Earn Your Potential?

Do you have Drive, Initiative, and Self Discipline?
We are looking for someone who can say YES!

We are one of Canada's leading widget producers, with an excellent reputation for customer service. We are offering an exciting career opportunity in our Toronto branch for an Account Manager.

A new business developer, with a proven track record of exceeding sales objectives, the successful candidate understands how to create new business and acquire new customers, while always maintaining a strong customer solution orientation when servicing existing accounts.

To the right individual, we are offering an uncapped performance based compensation package with an extremely competitive base, an automobile and cell phone allowance, a full benefits package, comprehensive training, and a protected territory.

The successful candidate must have a proven track record of success. In addition, he/she will possess:
- A post-secondary education.
- A minimum of 3 to 5 years business to business sales experience.
- Basic computer skills, including Word, Excel and email.
- Bilingual in French and English is a definite asset.
- A valid driver's license as travel within a designated district territory is required.

Please email your resume to: candidates@widgetproducer.com.

We thank all applicants that apply, however only those chosen for an interview will be contacted.

Other Recruiting Alternatives

Instead of advertising for sales candidates yourself, one option is to outsource the whole process and hire a professional recruiter to find your sales talent. This is a viable option for many organizations as long as the recruiter is experienced and specialized in sales recruiting. Otherwise, the recruiter is no more qualified to find your sales talent than you are, just much more expensive. Also, since a recruiter only gets paid when you hire their candidate, they can often inundate you with candidates and push you into making a decision you may regret after their 90 day guarantee expires.

Many recruiting firms find their candidates by simply searching through the resumes listed on the mega job boards. They then contact the candidates, conduct brief interviews and pass along the best resumes to their clients. While some sales organizations find this to be a huge time saver, others do not have the budget to spend 10 to 20 percent of a sales professional's first year compensation package on someone who essentially just searches through an online resume database.

To save the cost of a recruiter, another option is to pay to search the online resume databases yourself. Depending on the database, this can be very expensive, take many hours to search, and still yield few results. Some databases boast that they have millions of resumes on file, but when you drill down in your searches, you find that many of them are either very old and out of date, or not relevant to your candidate search. In some cases, candidates posted their resumes years earlier, and are no longer available on the job market, but the resume remains in the database to "beef up" the stats. You could waste a good portion of your recruiting budget buying access to millions of useless resumes when all you really need is one good one.

An excellent source of sales candidates is right outside your office door. Instead of paying a recruiter, why not pay a finder's fee to anyone in your organization that refers a potential candidate to you that turns into a successful hire. Not only will you have filled an open territory, but you will be building company loyalty as well.

We stated earlier that it is extremely unlikely that you have qualified potential sales candidates banging down your front door begging to work for you. While that's true, chances are you do have qualified sales candidates banging down your door trying to sell you something. Always take the time to speak with every telemarketer who calls and with every sales representative who knocks on your door. Tell everyone in your organization to do the same. Opportunity in the form of your next quota buster may be knocking, but you still have to open the door. After all, if that sales representative got through your door, he can probably get through your prospective customer's door as well. Not only could you find your next sales professional this way, but you will have also conducted the first interview in your screening process.

Making The Right Choice

As stated earlier, making the wrong sales hire can be very expensive. While you can never be 100 percent sure that you are hiring the right candidate, you can significantly increase your chances if you prescreen the applicants correctly.

Reviewing Resumes

You probably don't have time to interview every candidate that applies for your position. In the end you want to hire the best candidate, but at this point in time, all you have to narrow the field of applicants is the information found on the resumes.

Resumes are the sales professional's brochure. Like any marketing piece, they are designed to sell you something. In this case, they are trying to sell you on the sales person themselves. Like all brochures, you must learn to look past the sales pitch and read the real story.

For example, the titles for previous positions held can be misleading. Even sales people with very little experience or without a proven track record of success have been known to hold titles such as "Director of Sales" or "Vice President of Sales" in very small or family run businesses. Look deeper to review the actual responsibilities and transferable skills that they developed in each position, as well as what they accomplished while performing them.

It is generally believed if a sales person was successful in one sales position, he or she can be successful in another. In other words, past history can be a good indicator of future performance. If a resume outlines quantifiable sales results, or lists sales awards and achievements earned, you will definitely want to interview that candidate. The same is true for a candidate who specifies their sales activities levels such as a certain number of cold calls or product presentations per week. Anyone can state that they are a "hard worker" or an "overachiever", but have they listed their quantifiable accomplishments to prove they can deliver?

Another clue as to how successful a sales candidate was at selling in the past is the length of tenure at each previous position. Most quota busting sales professionals stay at their jobs for an average of three to five years. On the other hand, if a previous job was held for a period of less than one year, the candidate was probably not successful while doing it. Chances are they either resigned because they were not making any money, or they were dismissed for lack of performance. Either way, a short tenured position is a warning sign that you need to watch for. If there are more than one of these listed on the resume, it is probably best to move on to the next candidate

A large gap of time between two employers is also a warning sign. Most successful sales people don't leave their current position unless they already have secured their new position. Gaps between two listed positions mean that this was not likely the case. Barring unforeseen circumstances like a company closure or lay off, this is a clue that the employment was terminated for one reason or another. Again, many of these gaps on a person's resume is an indication that perhaps the sales representative is better at selling themselves in an interview as opposed to actually selling product!

It is standard practice for candidates to list their education on their resumes. Once again, however you need again look past the sales pitch of the brochure. For example, if a degree is not listed after the university name, they may have attended the school, they just may not have graduated.

Some companies want to hire candidates with their specific industry experience. If this is one of your requirements, as you review all the resumes you have received, you may realize that these types of sales candidates can sometimes be hard to find. You should also have related industries in mind so that you will be able to recognize them as desirable when reviewing the resumes. For example, ask yourself, if sales success in your industry requires hunters and cold callers, then what other industries employ those types of sales people? Sometimes, related industry experience can be just as relevant as actual industry experience.

Other sections of the resume can also shed some light into the personality of the candidate. For example, professional designations and training courses from trade associations indicate that a candidate is open-minded and willing to learn. While it does not guarantee that the sales skills will be better than someone without them, designations like Certified Sales Professional or B2B Sales Connections Accreditation, especially when completed at the candidate's own expense, does show a dedication to their chosen profession, which is a very desirable quality in an employee.

Participation in sports and clubs, especially at a high level, not only shows that the candidate has a competitive nature, it also shows that he or she is dedicated and hard working as evidenced by the hours of practice required to excel. Committee memberships and volunteer work shows that the candidate is willing to do more than "just show up" so to speak, they are willing to work hard and give something extra for something they are passionate about.   If a candidate has been publicly recognized or received awards for their extra-curricular activities, they should definitely be added to your interview list.

On the other hand, if you receive a cover letter that is addressed to another company, it shows that the candidate may be lazy and will only put out enough effort just to get by. Not correcting spelling mistakes indicates that he or she does not care about the details. By not following the application process as you requested in your advertisement, the candidate has indicated that they may have an issue taking direction from a sales manager.

In the end, if you decide to interview someone because they looked great on their resume, but then did not turn out to be the right fit in the meeting, you have only lost some time. For example, if a resume shows that a person has the right experience, but doesn't show specific sales results, interview the candidate anyway and ask them directly about their sales performance.

When in doubt, grant the interview. You may just meet that diamond in the ruff who turns out to be your next quota buster.

Email & Telephone Prescreening

Before you take the time to meet with a candidate, you need to ensure that he or she meets the basic criteria of your position as outlined on your job description. The best way to do this is by asking the candidate direct questions, either by email or on the telephone, before arranging a face to face interview. Some online job board services like those offered by B2B Sales Connections will even do this for you, saving you time and effort in the recruiting process.

The questions you ask should be pre-planned and closed ended. The open ended questions should be saved for the face to face interview. They should be worded so the candidate can answer with either a yes or no, or their answers indicate whether they pass or fail your criteria. For example, if your available position requires the candidate to be fully bilingual, then you will want to confirm this skill right up front.

Some other questions you could ask in your interview pre-screening are as follows:

- What is your annual income expectation?
- What is the annual base salary that you require?
- How many years have you been in B2B sales?
- What is your highest level of education completed?
- Do you have a valid driver's license?
- Are you able to travel outside of the country for business purposes?

- In your ideal sales position, what portion of your selling time would be dedicated to new customer acquisition versus current account management?

You should ask a direct question for all of your minimum requirements. If the candidate does not meet your requirements, then there is no point in taking them further into the selection process. For example, one sales manager was asked in the first two minutes of an interview if the position was solely a new customer acquisition role, as the candidate asking was not interested in those types of positions. "Yes it is," said the manager. "Thanks for coming in." and the interview was terminated right there and then.

If you have an absolute requirement, there is no point in you wasting your time interviewing someone who does not have it. If they do meet all your criteria however, you are another step closer to finding your ideal candidate.

Conducting Interviews

Now that you have selected the best resumes and narrowed the field by asking qualifying questions by either telephone or email, the next step in the prescreening process is to meet with each of the candidates for a face to face interview. The key to conducting a good interview, one that really lets you get to know the candidate, their skills and their fit to your organization, is planning. A meeting that only regurgitates what is listed on the resume will not help you find your perfect candidate any more than throwing darts at a dart board will.

Where ever possible, schedule your interviews one after another, booked an hour apart. It is much easier to compare the candidates when you see them one after the other. Also, you may want each candidate to interview with more than one person in your company. Those who are successful in the first meeting can then immediately proceed to the next. Like many things in life, when hiring a sales professional, it sometimes helps to get a second opinion.

As every candidate is different, if you just let the direction of the meeting go wherever the conversation takes you, it will be like comparing apples to oranges when trying to decide whom to hire. Besides, having a chat about the local sports teams will not guarantee you make the right hire. In order to properly compare and evaluate the candidates in an interview, you need to ask the same questions of each and every one, and those questions must be scripted a head of time.

When you completed the *Ideal Sales Candidate Definition Worksheet*, you identified the top personality traits that could be used to describe your ideal sales professional. In your first interview, you want to ask a question that will give you insight into those desired traits. For example, if you want someone who is competitive, you could ask each candidate to describe themselves in a competitive situation. Another example is if one of your desired traits is to be self-motivated, you could ask how the candidates keep themselves motivated.

By asking each candidate the same question as it relates back to your ideal candidate definition, you will weeding out the irrelevant information and only assessing what is important to you when making the right hiring decision for your available position.

Shown on the next page is an example of an effective first interview script for a sales position. The ideal candidate being interviewed in this example needs to be hard working and self-disciplined in a role that is mostly new customer acquisitions. The desired candidate should be self-motivated and have a desire to grow within the organization. Lastly, they need to be organized and have a proven track record of sales success. As you can see from the scripted questions, when all the first interviews are over, it would be very easy to compare and evaluate all the candidates on the required criteria.

Note the opening greeting references that you are trying to create a win - win relationship between the organization and the candidate. It is important to state this as your purpose of the meeting. There are no right or wrong answers, at this point you are just getting to know each other. By letting them know this is your purpose at the outset, you are creating a more relaxed atmosphere where the candidate will likely be more open with you.

FIRST INTERVIEW SCRIPT

Opening Statement

Hi, my name is _____, Regional Sales Manager. The purpose of our meeting today is to get to know each other better to see whether we would be a good fit; a win – win relationship. Does this sound good to you?

Interview Questions

1. Tell me about your current position; just a brief outline of your major responsibilities.
   a. What are the measurements of successful performance in the job? How well did you meet them?
   b. Repeat for other positions listed on resume.
2. What were the keys to your sale success in the past?
3. Describe a typical day. Describe a typical week?
4. Describe how you generate new customers?
5. Describe how you organize yourself. If you were prospecting and you received 10 business cards, only 1 of which could do business with you today, what would you do with the other 9 cards?
6. If I called your current sales manager, what would they say about you?
7. What motivates you?
8. What are your income expectations? How much would be salary, and how much would be performance based?
9. Describe where you would like to be in 5 years?
10. Do you prefer a lot of structure in your work environment, or do you like to work on your own?
11. How often do you seek your manager's time?
12. How do you feel when you win a sale? When you lose?
13. What led you to interview with us?
14. Describe you ideal sales position.
15. If you were interviewing for 2 positions, each with identical compensation, how would you determine which to choose?

Closing

That is all the questions that I have for now. Do you have any questions?

Could you leave me with a list of references today? Thanks for your time.

Also, a true sales professional knows that only the right fit will work in the long run, and is therefore interviewing you as much as you are interviewing them. Therefore, as scripted in the example, you must give them the opportunity to ask you questions at the end of the interview as well. By doing so, you will be able to further assess what is important to the candidate and what they are looking for in a position. In fact, sometimes the candidate's questions give you more insight into a potential fit with the organization than your questions do.

After the first interviews are completed and you have graded each prospective employee, you should be able to further narrow down your list of potential candidates. Now you can conduct a second round of interviews with your short list. Only those candidates that meet your minimum acceptable levels in relation to your ideal sales candidate should continue in the pre screening process.

The second interview is more personal and tailored to the candidate than the first interview. If there were any warning signs that resulted from the candidate's resume or from the initial meeting, these should be clarified here. Any subject like sales results or previous employment history that needs clarification should be addressed.

Also, it is recommended that you conduct a few role play scenarios with your candidates in the second interview. You could ask them to perform a prospecting call, or to try and interest you in the product they are currently selling. There is no better way to assess the current sales skills of an applicant than to see them in action.

Checking References

Even if you think you have just interviewed your perfect sales candidate and are ready to make an offer of employment, you still should make every effort, by whatever means possible, to ensure that they are who they say they are by conducting thorough reference check.

This can be accomplished three ways. The best way is to have the candidate arrange in advance for their references to expect your telephone call at a specific date and time. Secondly, you can try and reach the supplied references within a specific time frame. Finally, you can hire a professional organization that specializes in this area to conduct the reference interviews for you. Regardless of the method, you should always take the time to complete the reference checks before you formally offer the sales person a job.
Some employers do not believe in checking a potential sales candidate's references. They believe that no one would provide the name of a bad reference, so why bother waste the time to contact them. While this is true, when the review process is planned and executed

properly, references can give you valuable insight into a candidate's skills and personality that you cannot find anywhere else.

For example, most candidates already have a list of three references prepared when they arrive for their interview. While this is a good place to start, often these references can be of a personal nature, as opposed to work related. In addition to their prepared list, ask the candidate for at least three names of past supervisors, co-workers or colleagues that they have worked with in the past that you could also contact. If a candidate cannot provide at least three names and phone numbers for work related references, you should think twice before hiring them.

Once you have your list of references, the next step is to call them. Just like your candidate interviews, you need to ask the same questions on each of your reference interviews, and those questions must be scripted a head of time.

The *Candidate Reference Check Form* shown on the next page will ensure that you ask all the right questions to each reference contacted. As you will be asking the same questions to all, not only will it be very easy to compare the answers given by each reference on the same candidate, but across candidates as well.

CANDIDATE REFERENCE CHECK FORM

Candidate Name: _____

Position Applied For: _____

Date Of Reference Check: _____

Reference Name: _____

Reference Title: _____

Relationship To The Candidate: _____

Employment Start Date: _____

Employment End Date: _____

What was the reason the candidate left the position? _____
_____
_____

What were the candidate's primary responsibilities? _____
_____
_____
_____

How were the measurements for successful performance in the position? _____
_____
_____
_____

How well did the candidate meet them? _____
_____
_____
_____

How would you describe the candidate's personality? _____

_____

_____

_____

What are the candidate's strengths? _____

_____

_____

_____

What are the candidate's weaknesses? _____

_____

_____

_____

How did the candidate interact with other employee's? _____

_____

_____

_____

How did the candidate interact with management? _____

_____

_____

_____

Is there anything that I should keep in mind when training the candidate? _____

_____

_____

Would you rehire the candidate? _____

_____

_____

Are there any other comments? _____

_____

_____

_____

Another way to check a candidate's references is by asking for copies of reference letters. While no candidate will ever give you a copy of a bad reference letter, and you need to keep in mind that in some cases the candidate has written the letter and just asked for the reference to sign it, they still can be a source of valuable insight into the candidate and their skills. If nothing else, it is another way to obtain a name and phone number of someone you can call and complete a thorough reference check as discussed above.

References do not have to always be provided directly by the applicant. If you know someone at their previous employer, ask their opinion on your potential hire. Use your business contacts and networks to research the candidate. Under no circumstances, however, should you ask someone at the candidate's current employer without their permission. They have applied to you in confidence and you have no right to inform their current employer that they are in the process of making a career change.

Other Decision Tools

Sales aptitude testing is becoming more and more popular as a means to further assess your short list of potential sales candidates. These assessments are quick and easy for the candidate to complete online and are very inexpensive. Once finished, you receive a report outlining information such as the candidate's strengths, weaknesses, personality description and what type of sales would suit them best. This is very helpful to confirm what you think you discovered in the interview processes. You also could learn important information as to how to better structure your training programs should you end up hiring the candidate, so that your new sales professional will be more productive, faster.

Some companies place such a high value on aptitude testing that they will only interview candidates after they complete the aptitude assessment and meet certain personality criteria. This is not a recommended practice. Not only may you prematurely dismiss a qualified candidate, but it could also get to be very expensive to test everyone that walks through the door.

Never base your hiring decision solely on aptitude and personality tests. Even the most reputable sales testing firms will tell you that the test results should only account for no more than 25 percent of your hiring decision. A better plan is to only test your short list of candidates that successfully completed your interview process.
You should also do an internet search on the candidate. This can be as easy as entering the candidate's name into a few search engines like Google. In this case, no news is good news. Also, search the online social networks like LinkedIn™ or Facebook™. If your potential sales candidates are registered, their online profiles can be very revealing.

Lastly, depending on the available position and your industry, you may need to do a very detailed background checks on your potential employees. This could include criminal record checks, driver's license validations, credit histories, educational background confirmations, or even drug testing. If any of these tests may be applicable to your situation, first seek legal council to determine what is acceptable in your province or state. Then, as these checks can be very complicated, it is recommended to hire an outside firm who specializes in the types of services you need. It only takes one law suit to make up for any savings you would have realized by doing these tests yourself.

Making The Offer

With all the interviewing and prescreening complete, you now must make a choice. Contrary to popular belief, the choice is not which candidate will you hire, rather it's should you hire any of the candidates.

Remember, the wrong hire will be extremely costly to your organization. Don't make an offer just because you have an opening. It is better to have an open territory than to have bad representation. If you did not find the right fit this round, run your ads again. Waiting to hire the right sales professional will be less expensive to you in the long run than hiring the wrong candidate now.

On the other hand, some sales managers realize that finding the right sales people is so difficult that if they find two candidates that would fit, they hire them both, even if they only had one available position in the first place. If you believe you have found the right sales professional for you and your organization, make an offer and make it quickly. If your perfect fit was interviewing with you, chances are they were also interviewing with other sales organizations. Make the hiring decision today, as they may not be available tomorrow.

Continuing with the analogy that the employer employee relationship is like a marriage and the compensation plan is the marriage license that binds them, then the offer of employment is the prenuptial agreement finalized before the relationship begins. As with all such agreements, offers should not be made verbally, they need to be put in writing.

On the next page is a sample offer letter that can easily be customized for your situation. Please be sure to check with your own legal counsel before you create an offer letter. Employment contracts are legal documents and should be written by qualified professionals who are familiar with your local employment laws and regulations.

As you can see, your letter must include the details of compensation package, the general responsibilities and expectations of the position, as well as outline the conditions of employment. When both you and the candidate sign the offer, you are ensuring that both of you are on the same page right from the start of the relationship.

No one can be 100 percent sure that you are hiring the right candidate. Despite the manager's best efforts to prevent it in the prescreening process, sometimes candidates are just not who they said they were going to be, or they just didn't fit within the organization. Therefore you should always give yourself the option of ending the relationship within a specified period of time with no questions asked. To do this, you should always include a probationary period with terms similar to those in the sample offer letter.

When you make your offer of employment to your best candidate, don't tell the other acceptable candidates that you have done so. If your first choice rejects your offer, you can then present your offer to your second choice. Once your offer has been accepted by a candidate, however, etiquette dictates that you inform all the unsuccessful candidates that you interviewed that the position has been filled. This can be done either by email or telephone, depending on how far into the prescreening process the candidate was taken.

When informing these candidates, keep it professional, keep it positive and keep the door open for the future. Chances are that you will need to hire another sales professional sometime in the future. The best way to start is to cold call your own database of previously interviewed candidates whom you already classified as acceptable to see if they are interested in the position.

SAMPLE OFFER OF EMPLOYMENT LETTER

July 7, 2009

Samual A. Representative
123 Any Street
Toronto, ON
H0H 0H0

> **Disclaimer**: Always check with legal counsel before creating an offer of employment to insure you comply with your local labour & employment requirements.

Dear Sam:

On behalf of ABC Profit Limited, I am pleased to confirm our offer of employment to you for the position of Account Manager, reporting to Mathew Manager, Regional Sales Manager, servicing the Western GTA territory in the Toronto Branch, commencing on July 27, 2009.

The terms of this employment offer are as follows:

Compensation

Based on an annual sales quota of $750,000, your annual target gross income in this position will be $100,000, which includes an annual base salary of $40,000 and $60,000 of performance based income per year. You will receive a detailed copy of your compensation plan on your first day of employment.

You will receive your pay twice monthly on the 15th and 30th of each month.

Introductory Period

Your employment with ABC Profit Limited will begin with an introductory period of three (3) months. During this time, you will not hold a quota as you will be becoming acquainted with the responsibilities of your position. Also, you will receive a performance income guarantee in the amount of $15,000.

At the end of the three-month introductory period, your supervisor will evaluate your performance. If your performance does not meet acceptable levels, the company may terminate your employment without following a course of progressive discipline.

At the start of your fourth month, you will begin to carry your full sales quota and you will be compensated in accordance with the terms of your compensation plan.

Other Compensation

In addition to the above, you will be eligible to receive an automobile allowance in the amount of $500.00 per month and a cellular allowance of $200.00 per month.

You will be eligible for a comprehensive benefits program after three months of employment. A benefits enrolment kit will be provided to you on your first day.

You are eligible for three (3) weeks of vacation per year effective January 2010. In 2009, your vacation entitlement will be prorated and you will be entitled to 6.5 days.

Employment Conditions

This offer of employment is contingent upon your successful completion of all reference and background checks. An unfavorable result of a reference or a background investigation may result in the withdrawal of this employment offer.

Also, holding a valid driver's license is a condition of employment.

Acknowledgement

Please acknowledge your acceptance of this offer by signing below and returning it to me within two days.

I am pleased to make this offer to you, and I look forward to the opportunity to work with you. If you have any questions, please do not hesitate to contact me.

Sincerely,

Matthew Manager
Regional Sales Manager

_____

I accept this offer of employment with ABC Profit Limited as outlined above.

Name: _____ Signature: _____

Position Title: _____ Date: _____

CONCLUSION

Building a successful sales organization starts with building a successful sales team. However an eagle in one nest could just be a turkey in another. A sales manager, with many candidates to choose from, must use all the tools at his disposal to choose wisely so that both the employer and the employee prosper.

"Great vision without great people is irrelevant." – Jim Collins

APPENDIX – MANUAL CALCULATION FORMS

For those of you who are not familiar with Excel spreadsheets, all the calculations discussed in this training module can also be done manually. Simply print the forms on the following pages and follow the instructions.

Excel is a very common business software program. It is highly recommended that you take the time to learn the basics. Not only will you find that it can make your life much easier, you will find it to be a very profitable business tool as well.

JOB DESCRIPTION FORM - SALES

Division/Department: _____

Position Title: _____

Position Reporting To: _____

Position Type: _____

Location Where Position Will Be Based: _____

Geographic Description of Territory Assignment: _____

Travel Requirements: _____

General Job Description: _____
_____
_____

Work Experience Requirements: _____

Education Requirements: _____

Other Requirements: _____
_____
_____

Annual Sales Quota: _____

Other Performance Targets: _____
_____

Percentage of Time to Be Spent on New Customer Acquisition: _____

Target Income at Quota: _____ Base Salary: _____

Other Compensation Included: _____

Ideal Sales Candidate
Definition Worksheet

Enter the names of your top 4 sales professionals in the space provided. Then select their top personality traits that describe them by putting a "Y" in the appropriate box. Total the number of times a personality trait has occurred in the Ideal Sales Candidate column.

Common Sales Personality Trait	Name of Sales Professional #1:	Name of Sales Professional #2:	Name of Sales Professional #3:	Name of Sales Professional #4:	Name of Sales Professional #5:	Ideal Sales Candidate - Total of Personality Trait Occurances
Action Oriented						
Ambitious						
Analytical						
Assertive						
Coachable						
Competitive						
Composed						
Creative						
Curious						
Diciplined						
Direct						
Driven						
Empathetic						
Energetic						
Enthusiatic						
Entrepreneurial						
Ethical						
Focused						
Good Listener						
Grounded						
Hard Working						
Honest						
Independent						
Money Motivated						
Open Minded						
Optimistic						
Organized						
Outgoing						
Persistant						
Personable						
Persuasive						
Results Oriented						
Self Confident						
Self Motivated						
Tough Minded						

FIRST INTERVIEW SCRIPT

Opening Statement

Hi, my name is _____, Regional Sales Manager. The purpose of our meeting today is to get to know each other better to see whether we would be a good fit; a win – win relationship. Does this sound good to you?

Interview Questions

1. Tell me about your current position; just a brief outline of your major responsibilities.
   a. What are the measurements of successful performance in the job? How well did you meet them?
   b. Repeat for other positions listed on resume.
2. What were the keys to your sale success in the past?
3. Describe a typical day. Describe a typical week?
4. Describe how you generate new customers?
5. Describe how you organize yourself. If you were prospecting and you received 10 business cards, only 1 of which could do business with you today, what would you do with the other 9 cards?
6. If I called your current sales manager, what would they say about you?
7. What motivates you?
8. What are your income expectations? How much would be salary, and how much would be performance based?
9. Describe where you would like to be in 5 years?
10. Do you prefer a lot of structure in your work environment, or do you like to work on your own?
11. How often do you seek your manager's time?
12. How do you feel when you win a sale? When you lose?
13. What led you to interview with us?
14. Describe you ideal sales position.
15. If you were interviewing for 2 positions, each with identical compensation, how would you determine which to choose?

Closing

That is all the questions that I have for now. Do you have any questions?

Could you leave me with a list of references today? Thanks for your time.

CANDIDATE REFERENCE CHECK FORM

Candidate Name: _____

Position Applied For: _____

Date Of Reference Check: _____

Reference Name: _____

Reference Title: _____

Relationship To The Candidate: _____

Employment Start Date: _____

Employment End Date: _____

What was the reason the candidate left the position? _____
_____
_____

What were the candidate's primary responsibilities? _____
_____
_____
_____

How were the measurements for successful performance in the position? _____
_____
_____
_____

How well did the candidate meet them? _____
_____
_____
_____

How would you describe the candidate's personality? _____

_____

_____

What are the candidate's strengths? _____

_____

_____

_____

What are the candidate's weaknesses? _____

_____

_____

_____

How did the candidate interact with other employee's? _____

_____

_____

_____

How did the candidate interact with management? _____

_____

_____

_____

Is there anything that I should keep in mind when training the candidate? _____

_____

_____

Would you rehire the candidate? _____

_____

_____

Are there any other comments? _____

_____

_____

_____

SAMPLE OFFER OF EMPLOYMENT LETTER

July 7, 2009

Samual A. Representative
123 Any Street
Toronto, ON
H0H 0H0

> **Disclaimer**: Always check with legal counsel before creating an offer of employment to insure you comply with your local labour & employment requirements.

Dear Sam:

On behalf of ABC Profit Limited, I am pleased to confirm our offer of employment to you for the position of Account Manager, reporting to Mathew Manager, Regional Sales Manager, servicing the Western GTA territory in the Toronto Branch, commencing on July 27, 2009.

The terms of this employment offer are as follows:

Compensation

Based on an annual sales quota of $750,000, your annual target gross income in this position will be $100,000, which includes an annual base salary of $40,000 and $60,000 of performance based income per year. You will receive a detailed copy of your compensation plan on your first day of employment.

You will receive your pay twice monthly on the 15th and 30th of each month.

Introductory Period

Your employment with ABC Profit Limited will begin with an introductory period of three (3) months. During this time, you will not hold a quota as you will be becoming acquainted with the responsibilities of your position. Also, you will receive a performance income guarantee in the amount of $15,000.

At the end of the three-month introductory period, your supervisor will evaluate your performance. If your performance does not meet acceptable levels, the company may terminate your employment without following a course of progressive discipline.

At the start of your fourth month, you will begin to carry your full sales quota and you will be compensated in accordance with the terms of your compensation plan.

Other Compensation

In addition to the above, you will be eligible to receive an automobile allowance in the amount of $500.00 per month and a cellular allowance of $200.00 per month.

You will be eligible for a comprehensive benefits program after three months of employment. A benefits enrolment kit will be provided to you on your first day.

You are eligible for three (3) weeks of vacation per year effective January 2010. In 2009, your vacation entitlement will be prorated and you will be entitled to 6.5 days.

Employment Conditions

This offer of employment is contingent upon your successful completion of all reference and background checks. An unfavorable result of a reference or a background investigation may result in the withdrawal of this employment offer.

Also, holding a valid driver's license is a condition of employment.

Acknowledgement

Please acknowledge your acceptance of this offer by signing below and returning it to me within two days.

I am pleased to make this offer to you, and I look forward to the opportunity to work with you. If you have any questions, please do not hesitate to contact me.

Sincerely,

Matthew Manager
Regional Sales Manager
_____

I accept this offer of employment with ABC Profit Limited as outlined above.

Name: _____ Signature: _____

Position Title: _____ Date: _____

Chapter 3 – It All Starts Here!
Your 90 Day Sales Rep Success Plan

"Failures don't plan to fail; they fail to plan." –
Harvey Mackay

YOUR ROAD MAP TO SUCCESS

Imagine you were visiting a new city for the first time. You are in your rental car sitting in the airport parking lot and you need to drive across town to a very important business meeting. The only tool you have to help you is that you know how to drive because you have done it before. What else will you need to make the meeting on time?

At the very minimum, you will need the car keys and sufficient gas in the tank. Otherwise the car is completely useless to you, even with your previous driving experience. Some sort of navigation device like a map or GPS would also be very helpful. You may be lucky enough to find your way to the meeting without one of these aids, but you would probably waste a lot of time driving in circles before you found your way.

Now, think about the last time you welcomed a new sales representative to work at your company. Did you have a pre-determined road map in place that pointed them in the right direction from day one, or was it more like, "Welcome to the company. Here's your price book, now go out and sell." If you answered the latter, you basically left your new sales representative in the airport parking lot with nothing but the car keys!

You Need A Plan

A sales representative without a success plan is like a ship without a rudder. He will spend a lot of time sailing in circles, but will never really get closer to where he wants to go. A sales representative with a success plan but no plan of action to follow is like a ship's captain without a navigational map. He may be lucky enough to be sailing in a straight line, but he may be sailing in the wrong direction.

As a sales manager, you must ensure that your team is sailing straight, and in the right direction from the first moment they walk through your door. The only way to accomplish this is with a structured, documented "on boarding process".

Unfortunately, most sales managers don't have a structured process for orientating new hires to the company. Instead, many sales representatives are hired and then pretty much left on their own. They end up wasting time trying to figure out what to do and how to do it. This sink or swim philosophy is a very bad way to start a new business relationship. The sales representative becomes frustrated and unproductive, and the disappointed sales manager wonders if he made the wrong hiring decision in the first place.

To prevent this, you need a plan. You need a detailed on boarding process to put your sales representatives on the right path from day one. Then, instead of the sales representative spinning their wheels at the start, they will have spent their time productively because they have spent it selling.

Even if you are not hiring anyone new in the near future, you still need to create your plan for your existing sales team. Treat tomorrow as their day one! The sooner they get on the right path, the sooner you all will be successful. Whether you are working with a new hire or an existing employee that is not performing to their potential, you need to create a sales process that defines the fastest way to make your sales representative profitable. This section of the training course will give you the framework to do so.

YOUR 90 DAY SALES REP SUCCESS PLAN

A Sales Rep Success Plan must be detailed, specific, and customized to the product or service that you sell, and for the operating procedures of your company.   It should also cover a specified time frame.

Specifically, your Sales Rep Success Plan should include the following:

- Company Orientation
- Human Resources Procedures
- Compensation Plan Review
- Product Training
- Sales Training
- Customer Relationship Management (CRM) System Training
- Order Processing Training
- Company Procedure Training
- Performance Expectations and Monitoring

Your Sales Rep Success Plan is essentially a detailed road map to success for your entire sales team to follow. The more detailed the road map, the greater the chances for success.

Company Orientation

Customers will only do business with companies they can trust. They need to know that you can service their needs. As a sales manager, your sales representatives are your customers. They will only work for companies they can trust and they need to know that you can help them fulfill their personal needs. This trust begins to develop from the moment you introduce the company to your new employee.

You should always commit to spending at least a couple of hours with your new hire first thing in the morning on their first day of work. Book this off like an appointment, and do not let any last minute distractions get in the way.

The purpose of the Company Orientation is for the new employee to get to know the company and its people. The best way to start this is to conduct a facility tour. Although this may sound very basic, it is very important. Every new employee needs to know the lay of the land. This can include many of the simple things we take for granted. Where to hang their coat, which desk is theirs, the location of the lunch room, information on the company dress code, finding office supplies, washrooms, even where to park their car. These are all very important questions that need to be answered. Also, be sure to point out important "need to know" information such as restricted areas in the building or the all important how to work the coffee machine. Although some of this may seem trivial, it is this kind of detail that lets a new hire know you are interested in their well being and success.

Every new employee needs to know about the people they will be interacting with and what roles they play in relation to their sales position. They need to know who to go to, when, so to speak. As such, it is important not to leave employee introductions to chance. Instead of just "Jane, this is Jack", every introduction on your tour should have a purpose. "Jane, this is Jack, our new sales representative covering the Eastern territory. You two will be working closely together since Jane processes all the orders from your territory."

Don't just introduce the company to the new employee, but also introduce the new employee to the company. A few days prior to them starting work, you should distribute a company wide memo or email introducing the new sales representative, their start date, their role within the company and a brief biography. Make sure you give a copy to the new employee before they start so they know what information has been released. As the tour proceeds and the new sales representative is introduced to the existing employees, trust and credibility will be built every time the new employee hears comments like, "Welcome! I heard you were joining the company today."

After your tour is over, you should meet with your new sales representative to finish the Company Orientation. Most sales presentations to prospective customers include some sort of information about your company. You should also give that same presentation to your new hire. You could include a brief company history, a sample client list, and information on why customers do business with you.

Added to your regular customer presentation, you should also include a company organization chart, outlining the reporting structure for the entire company. As your new hire would have just met many of the people listed on your tour, this will give them a very clear picture of each person's position and role within the organization.

Lastly, you should discuss what happens next. You should review your 90 Day Sales Rep Success Plan with your new sales representative and provide them with a copy. By reviewing the Success Plan, you are establishing shared expectations between you and your new hire and you are building trust. Nothing is left to interpretation. More importantly, you are giving your new employee the knowledge and confidence that your organization has a plan and intends to help them succeed.

Human Resource Procedures

New employees generate paperwork. There is just no way to avoid it, so it is best to get this task done as soon as possible and be done with it. Payroll forms, group insurance forms, non-disclosure forms and emergency contact forms are just a few of what may be required to work at your company. You should have a checklist of all the paperwork that a new hire must complete so that nothing is missed.

You should also create a list of any other information, tools, or equipment that will be issued to your sales representative. Anything that is assigned to the person individually should be included.

Although your final Basic Equipment List would be specific to your company, it could include:

- Keys to the office
- Security alarm code
- Long distance dialing code
- Long distance calling card
- Email address set up
- Computer or laptop assignment
- Cell phone or PDA assignment
- Computer and server login codes
- Employee phone and email directory
- Business cards
- Price book
- Customer lists
- Prospect lists
- Product demonstration kit
- Training Manuals

For items like laptop computers and cell phones, you want to outline if personal use is acceptable, or whether the equipment is to be used only for business purposes. You also want to be very clear as to who actually owns the equipment, and what happens should employment end. This is also true for proprietary company property like price books, demonstration kits, and customer lists. If applicable, you should have the employee sign an *Asset Tracking Worksheet* for each asset that will remain company property should employment end. You and the employee should each receive and file a copy of the signed form. An example of the form is shown below.

B B SALES CONNECTIONS

ASSET TRACKING FORM

I acknowledge receipt of the following asset:

Asset Description: ____Laptop Computer_____

Make: ____Dell_____

Model: ____Inspiron 1501_____

Serial Number: ____123-456-789-SAE_____

I understand that the use of this asset is for business purposes only.

I understand that this asset remains the property of ___ABC Profit Limited___.

I agree that this asset will be returned to the company upon request or termination of employment.

Employee: ____Samual A Representative_____

Department: ____Toronto Branch_____

Date: ____May 7, 2009_____

Employee's Signature: ____*Sam. A. Representative*_____

Manager's Signature: ____*Mathew Manager*_____

It is best to have as much of your Basic Equipment List ordered beforehand so that it is ready for distribution on the first day of employment. The sooner a sales representative has an email address and business cards, the sooner they can start selling!

Compensation Plan Review

A Compensation Plan Review is one of the most important meetings you can have with your sales representatives, and should be scheduled very soon after they start to work at your company. Every sales representative on your team must have a complete understanding as to how and when they are paid.

Have you ever heard, "let's not worry about how you are paid until you make a few sales and earn some commission!" If you ever find yourself saying this, or even thinking this, stop and think again. If a member of your team does not understand the compensation plan, it will be a constant distraction until they do.

Every company pays their sales staff differently. Designing a proper sales compensation plan was discussed previously in section 2 of this training course. At this point, it is important to note that salaries, bonuses, commissions, benefits, vacation allowances and expense reimbursements are just some of the components that can make up a sales compensation plan, and it is important that your representatives understand every aspect. They need to know when they will receive payment, and when they will not.

In your Compensation Plan Review, you should also discuss the sales representative's territory assignments; either designated by product and/or geography, and the process to resolve any disputes should they occur. Nothing will create animosity faster within your team than one sales representative selling in another sales person's territory.

Finally, you should also talk about when compensation is paid. For example, do you pay commissions when the product is installed or when the customer pays his invoice? Depending on the length of your sales cycle, the timing of when compensation becomes payable can make a huge difference as to when the sales representative will be paid.

Sales professionals by nature tend to be income oriented, competitive people. That is one reason why they thrive on performance based compensation. You must take the time in your Compensation Plan Review to ensure that you and your sales representatives are on the same page on this when it comes to compensation. Otherwise, there will be misunderstandings in the future, and these misunderstandings will only get in the way of more important things like making sales!

It is strongly recommended that you give your new sales representative a copy of their Compensation Plan in writing, and that they sign it to acknowledge they have received it and understand it using the *Compensation Plan Acknowledgement Form*. An example is shown below.

B SALES CONNECTIONS

COMPENSATION PLAN
ACKNOWLEDGEMENT FORM

I acknowledge that I have received and understand the contents of my Sales

Compensation Plan received from _____ABC Profit Limited_____.

Employee: _____Samual A. Representative_____

Department: _____Toronto Branch_____

Date: _____May 7, 2009_____

Employee's Signature: _____Sam A. Representative_____

Manager's Signature: _____Mathew Manager_____

Once your sales representative understands his compensation plan, you must relate it to their personal goals. People do not work for you, they work for themselves. The employment opportunity you provide is just a means to an end for what sales representatives want out of life. The career they have chosen is the way that they earn an income to fund their lifestyle. That desired lifestyle is a personal decision, and it requires a certain income to support it. The key as their sales manager is you must ensure that your career opportunity allows them to earn it.

This may be sounding somewhat familiar to you. That is good because it should! Just as you defined your personal goals in Section 1 of this training course, you sales representatives should define their goals using the *Personal Goal Definition Worksheet*. Then each member of your team should also take the time to convert their income goal into the daily activities required to earn it by reversing the sales process using the *Goal Setting & Action Planning Worksheet*.

B2B SALES CONNECTIONS

Goal Setting & Action Planning Worksheet

Enter data in yellow boxes to calculate the daily activities required to achieve your goals.

What is the total annual income you wish to earn to fund your lifestyle?	$ 100,000.00
What is your base salary?	$ 50,000.00
What is your average monthly bonus earned?	$ 500.00
What is your average commission rate?	8%
What is your average size sale?	$ 10,000.00
How many presentations does it take you to make a sale?	3.0
How many fact finds does it take you to make a presentation?	2.0
How many prospecting calls does it take you to book a fact find?	15.0
Total Annual Sales Volume Required for Goal Attainment	$ 550,000.00
Total Monthly Sales Volume Required for Goal Attainment	$ 45,833.33
Number of Sales Required Per Month	5
Number of Sales Required Per Week	1.25
Number of Presentations Required Per Month	15
Number of Presentations Required Per Week	3.75
Number of Fact Finds Required Per Month	30
Number of Fact Finds Required Per Week	7.50
Number of Prospecting Calls Required Per Month	450
Number of Prospecting Calls Required Per Week	113
Number of Prospecting Calls Required Per Day	23

When completing this worksheet with a new employee, they will not yet know the activity averages required to complete this sheet. You should therefore provide them with a copy of your team's averages so they can get things started based on true company numbers.

As you can see, to complete this worksheet, the new sales representative must have a thorough understanding of their compensation plan. Without it, it is very difficult to convert the achievement of their personal income goal into the daily activities required to earn it.

Over time, as the new sales representative tracks their sales activities using tools we will examine later, their own averages will emerge. As such, it is recommended that the *Goal Setting & Action Planning Worksheet* be revisited and adjusted at least every 90 days throughout the new employee's first year. That way they will always know what is required for them to reach their goals.

The Compensation Plan Review is one of the most important meetings you will have with your new hire. Not only does it show them how they will achieve their personal goals, it will also build the foundation of why they are working with you in the first place.

Product Training Schedule

Obviously, product knowledge is critical for your new hire's success. After all, every sales representative must understand the product or service they are selling, otherwise they couldn't sell it. The mistake most sales managers make however, is overestimating how much product knowledge a sales representative actually needs. More is definitely not always better!

It is very common for sales managers to have a new sales representative spend the first week on the job memorizing all the features and specifications of every product they are going to sell. This will not make your new sales representative better or more successful. In fact, speaking from personal experience, this will actually do more to confuse your new sales representative than it will to help them.

Besides, chances are that they won't be able to remember this technical information when compressed into such a short period of time. In fact, sales people tend to only remember product knowledge when they have a vested interest in doing so. In a nutshell, until they can see the information is important to a customer, it won't be important to your sales representative. Therefore, don't clutter their brains with facts and specifications that can be referenced later.

It is important to ensure that all technical information given is from a sales value point of view. Don't discuss features and specifications without directly relating them to the benefits they provide the customer. For example, stating that a machine operates at 60 cycles per minute is just useless trivia unless the customer has identified the need and will benefit from faster cycle speeds. If a feature does not yield a benefit to the customer, then as a general rule of thumb, the sales representative doesn't need to know it.

Your product knowledge training should start with a discussion of common industry terms. These would be terms or product features that are unfamiliar to someone new to your industry, but are not unique to your company or to the products that you sell. For example, if you have just joined the photocopier industry, you may not know what the term "automatic document feeder" means, however virtually every copier has one, so it is definitely a common industry term that your sales representatives would need to know.

In some cases, common industry features are not available on every model or product that you sell. Certain options may be available on some, they may be standard on others, or they may not be available at all on others. To continue the example from above, very small copiers may not have an automatic document feeder, whereas all medium and high volume copiers would. After a sales representative learns about the feature is, it is much easier to remember what model has it.

Once your sales representative has an understanding of your common industry terms and where in your product line they are available, you can then proceed to how your company and its products are unique in the marketplace. To continue the example from above, once your new sales person knows more about an automatic document feeder, the next step would be to learn why a customer would prefer your automatic document feeder over your competitor's.

As you can see, knowing why a customer would prefer your solution requires an understanding of your competition. To be successful, your sales representatives need to know not only your strengths in the marketplace, but they also need to know your weaknesses. What exclusive features do you have, what are your competitive advantages, and where are you vulnerable? It is best that your new sales representative know the real facts now, than to be broadsided later.

Have your sales team collect information so that you can create a competitive information library. File it by the competitor's name and model number, and keep it in a common area, so that everyone has access to it. You should also create a file that lists all of your competitor's websites and provide it in your training program so your new sales people can do research on their own.

When planning your product knowledge training, it is best to spread it out over a specific period of time. Your exact schedule will vary depending on your industry and the products you sell, but it is best not to overload your new hire too soon. More information will be retained in eight one hour sessions, than one eight hour session.

For example, in the first week, the new sales representative might just read product brochures. In week two, they could read the operator manuals and complete some classroom or hands-on product training. In week three, there may be a ride along with you, a senior sales representative, or even a service technician. Then in week four the new sales representative would be using and demonstrating the product on their own.

The spreadsheet *Product Training Schedule.xls* is an Excel workbook that will help you plan the product training of your new hire for their first 12 weeks of employment. For those of you not familiar with Excel, you can create the same schedule manually by using the forms found in Appendix A.

The first spreadsheet in the workbook, "Product Listing Worksheet" is a spreadsheet where you create your list of all possible product training topics, available trainers and training methods.

Product Listing Worksheet

B B SALES CONNECTIONS

Enter data in yellow boxes to create your Product Listing

Number	Product Training Topics	Available Trainers	Available Training Methods
1	Common Industry Terms	Self Study	Product Brochures
2	Widget 1	Senior Sales Rep	Operator Manuals
3	Widget 2	Sales Manager	Ride Along
4	Widget 3	Service Techician	Hands On
5		Administration	Classroom
6		Outside Training Company	Meeting
7		Corporate Trainer	Off Site Training Course
8		Other	
9			
10			
11			
12			

The second spreadsheet in the workbook, the "Product Training Schedule Worksheet", is where you actually start to develop your quarterly training schedule. The spreadsheet allows you to plan 50 separate product training events over the 12 week period. In each column where you are to enter data, drop down arrows appear when you select a cell. These drop downs include the lists you created earlier on the "Product Listing Worksheet". You simply click on your selection to enter the information. As you enter the information, the dates for the training will be automatically calculated from the start date, creating your customized training schedule.

The *Product Training Schedule.xls* spreadsheet can also be used for your existing sales representatives to plan their ongoing quarterly product training. It can be a very useful tool if you have a very technical product offering that requires more than 90 days of training to master, if you have a sales representative that needs a plan to improve their product knowledge, or if you launch new products on a regular basis.

You don't wait for all the stop lights to be green before you back your car out of the driveway every morning, and neither should your sales representatives! They don't need to know absolutely everything about a product before they can start selling it. If they get stopped by a red light because they don't know a piece of information, they can learn it then and turn the sales process light green again. Your goal is to give your team just enough sales focused product training so they can recognize a prospect when they see one.

Sales Training Schedule

The B2B sales process was discussed in detail in Section 1. As mentioned, the process contains three basic steps: prospecting, fact finding, and the presentation of offer stage. Each step leads to the next, where the intended end result is the completed sale.

Regardless of the level of experience the representative had before joining your company, you should always schedule sales training for your new hire in their first month of employment. Although they may have previous sales experience, chances are they have not sold your product or service before, and certainly not for your company. In order for them to become productive as quickly as possible, they will need sales training that is customized for your industry, your company, and your products.

Detailed information on how to customize the B2B sales process is the subject of the B2B Sales Connections training course, *Action Plan For Sales Success.* This course includes many automated tools to help you define your sales process and create the sales techniques your sales representatives will need to be successful. Although the course content will not be repeated in this sales management training program, we have included many of these automated workbooks for you to use. We hope you will find them very useful when training your sales representatives on your sales process.

Specifically included are:

- *Target Market Definition Worksheet* - It is wrong to believe that every company can and will buy your product or service. "Here are your business cards, there's a street. Now go out and sell." is a shot gun approach that requires more luck than sales skill. The fact of the matter is that where your sales team prospects is as important as how much they prospect. This detailed workbook will clearly define your target market so that your team will spend most of their time talking to prospects that are most likely to buy.

- *Prospecting Approach Worksheet* – Once your team knows what doors to knock on, they need to know the best way to open them! This worksheet will create an approach that includes all of the elements of an effective prospecting call.

- *Fact Find Creation Worksheet* – One of the most valuable lessons any sales professional can learn is that prospects buy for their own reasons, not the sales representative's. If your sales team can help their prospects get to where they want to go, or help them accomplish a specific goal, you all will be very successful in sales. To complicate things, different people buy the same product for completely different reasons. This worksheet will help you to create scripted questions so your team can determine who can buy, what product they will buy, and why they will buy it.

- *Presentation of Offer Planning Worksheet* – The key to an effective presentation of offer sales call is to give the prospect just the right amount of information so they can make the buying decision. The old saying, "too much information" also applies in sales. This workbook helps you to plan what information is necessary, and how it should be delivered. Separate worksheets are included for proposal template creation, demonstration planning, and closing interview preparation.

Who are the best prospects? What is the best prospecting approach to use? What questions should be asked of a potential customer? What is the best way to present your products so that the customer buys? The sooner your new sales representatives complete these worksheets, the sooner they can answer these questions, and the sooner they will start to sell.

As with your product training, spread your sales training over a specified period of time. Your exact schedule will vary depending on your industry and the products you sell, but again, it is best not to overload your new hire too soon.

When planning your training schedule remember to introduce one new section of the sales process at a time, starting with the new sales representative first learning the sales technique, then observing it being performed by someone else, then practicing the technique themselves.

For example, one week could be spent on nothing but prospecting. Your new hire could learn about the best prospects to target, what approaches work best, and how to file different prospects in their follow up file. They could also work with a senior sales representative so they can see the prospecting approach being performed in the field. By the end of that same week, with your guidance, your new hire could be completing prospecting calls in their own territory. The following week, while continuing the prospecting calls, the fact finding stage of the sales process could be introduced, with the presentation of offer stage the following week.

The spreadsheet *Sales Training Schedule.xls* is an Excel workbook that will help you plan the sales training of your new sales person for their first 12 weeks of employment. For those of you not familiar with Excel, you can create the same schedule manually by using the forms found in Appendix A.

The first spreadsheet in the workbook, "Sales Function Listing" is a spreadsheet where you create your list of all possible sales training topics, available trainers and training methods.

<table>
<tr><td colspan="4">**B** **SALES** CONNECTIONS</td><td colspan="1" align="right">**Sales Function Listing Worksheet**</td></tr>
<tr><td colspan="4" align="center">Enter data in yellow boxes to create your **Sales Function Listing**</td></tr>
</table>

Number	Sales Training Topics	Available Trainers	Available Training Methods
1	Target Market Definition	Self Study	Sales Self Study Guide
2	Follow Up File / CRM Training	Senior Sales Rep	Ride Along
3	Prospecting Approach	Sales Manager	Hands On
4	Fact Finding	Administration	Classroom
5	Presentation of Offer	Outside Training Company	Meeting
6		Corporate Trainer	Off Site Training Course
7		Other	
8			
9			
10			
11			
12			

The second spreadsheet in the workbook, the "Sales Training Schedule Worksheet", is where you start to develop your quarterly training schedule. It allows you to plan 50 separate sales training events over the 12 week period. In each column where you need to enter data, drop down arrows appear when you select a cell. These drop downs include the lists you created earlier in the "Sales Function Listing Worksheet". You simply click on your selection to enter the information. As you enter the information, the dates for the training will be automatically calculated from the start date, creating your customized schedule.

The *Sales Training Schedule.xls* workbook can also be used for your existing sales representatives to plan their ongoing quarterly sales training. It can be a very useful tool if you have a technical sales process that requires more than 90 days of training to master, if you have a sales representative that needs a plan to improve their sales skills, or if your product launches require updated sales training.

Sales Training Schedule Worksheet

Enter data in yellow boxes to create your Sales Training Schedule

| Trainee | Sam Sales Representative | | | Sales Training or Employment Start Date | | | 25-May-09 |

Week Number	Sales Function	Trainer	Training Method	Training Starts Week Of	Complete?	Notes
1	Target Market Definition	Self Study	Sales Self Study Guide	01-Jun-09	Yes	
1	Follow Up File / CRM Training	Sales Manager	Classroom	01-Jun-09	Yes	
2	Prospecting	Self Study	Sales Self Study Guide	08-Jun-09		
2	Prospecting	Senior Sales Rep	Ride Along	08-Jun-09		
2	Prospecting	Self Study	Practice	08-Jun-09		
3	Prospecting	Self Study	Practice	15-Jun-09		
3	Fact Finding	Self Study	Sales Self Study Guide	15-Jun-09		
3	Fact Finding	Sales Manager	Ride Along	15-Jun-09		
3	Fact Finding	Self Study	Practice	15-Jun-09		
4	Prospecting	Self Study	Practice	22-Jun-09		
4	Fact Finding	Self Study	Practice	22-Jun-09		
4	Presentation of Offer	Self Study	Sales Self Study Guide	22-Jun-09		
4	Presentation of Offer	Sales Manager	Ride Along	22-Jun-09		
4	Presentation of Offer	Self Study	Practice	22-Jun-09		

Think of your sales team as your professional sports franchise. You would not train your sports team by just lecturing your athletes on how to play, and then sending them into competition without ever having seen the game being played or having a chance to practice. If you wouldn't do it for your sports team, then don't do it for your sales team.

Instead, a great sports coach teaches the required skills, demonstrates them, and then allows the team to practice those skills until they became effortless, all the while giving immediate feedback. Your role as a sales manager is no different. It is only when your sales representatives put the sales theory into practice on a daily basis will they achieve positive sales results.

CRM System Training

A Follow-Up File or Customer Relationship Management (CRM) System is simply a must have in order to be successful in sales over the long term. Training on your CRM System is a sales function, and should be incorporated on your Sales Training Schedule as outlined above, however its importance cannot be understated, and therefore warrants a further discussion here.

In reality, there are only two ways for your sales representatives to make sales. One, they can sell to new customers, or two they can sell more products or services to existing customers. The key to realizing their true potential in the long term is to manage their customer relationships with a CRM System so that they can do both.

You may have already realized this and you are now one of the thousands of organizations currently using a CRM program. Before you skip to the next section, be careful. Just purchasing software is not enough. Even if your company currently uses a system, if it is not properly designed and managed, it is costing you and your sales representatives in lost opportunities.

To be effective, your CRM program must go beyond who bought what, when. It should also track all the elements that you use to define your target market such as your customer's industry and the size of their company. More importantly, it should track where every prospect is in the buying cycle.

Here is a true case in point. Over the course of a year, a local branch manager had seven separate photocopier sales people do face to face prospecting calls on her business. However, since the current equipment was on a lease with an expiry date far into the future, it was not the right time in the buying cycle for the company to be considered a prospect today. The branch manager asked each of the sales representatives to call back on the same specified date in the future. Of the seven representatives given this information on the timing of the next sale, only two called back! Only two!

Perhaps you are thinking that the sales representatives who didn't call back were no longer working for the same companies, and that is how the follow up dates were missed. If that is the case, then shame on those companies, who certainly rely on sales for survival, for not having a mechanism in place that tracked the buying cycles of all prospects, regardless of what sales representatives are covering the territory!

Although this case may seem unbelievable, unfortunately, it is more the rule, as opposed to the exception. In fact, it has been widely quoted in the sales industry that research shows 2 out of 3 sales are made to customers who have said no not once, but 5 times! It also shows that 63% of sales are made after the 5th rejection. Wasted opportunities like the example above stem from the fact that 75% of all sales people give up after the 1st or 2nd rejection. Given this, it certainly is easy to see why 25% of all sales representatives produce 90-95% of all sales! These are the representatives who use a Follow-Up File or CRM System and don't give up too early!

A Follow-Up File or CRM system can either be manual or an automated system, depending on the company, the type of products you sell, the user's preference and the sales person's level of computer skills. It can be as simple as 12 file folders with one for each month and each prospect filed by the next sales contact date, or an off the shelf software product costing a few hundred dollars, or as complicated as a complete customized solution, complete with web access, designed for your specific business or industry. Whatever type of system you use, the most important rule is to use it religiously.

While choosing a CRM software program is largely a function of preference and budget, whatever program you choose should have the following abilities:

- The ability to add user-defined fields. This will allow you to customize the program to ensure that you are tracking your target market characteristics.
- The ability to customize drop down lists within these user defined fields so you could just choose the data being entered as opposed to having to type it in for each record. Not only does this drastically speed data entry, but it also ensures the data is entered in exactly the same way each time, making it easier to search and analyze. More importantly, it eliminates the "garbage in, garbage out" syndrome that plagues so many CRM databases today.
- The ability to search the database across multiple fields. This function can be critical to ensure that your sales resources are being focused in the right place at the right time.
- The ability to make certain fields mandatory for data entry. This allows you to decide what critical information must be entered into the database in order for it to be accepted.
- The ability to have different security levels and user access controls. Giving everyone in your organization the ability to add and delete user-defined fields is just an accident of valuable information deletion waiting to happen. If everyone is allowed to delete files or other important data, there is always the chance that critical files can be deleted on mass either by mistake or on maliciously.
- As the sales manager, you need to ability to view your team's files at any given time and control their access. This lets you follow their progress, monitor their activity and deny access in case they leave your employment.

Once you have chosen your CRM System, the key is to ensure that your sales representatives actually use it. The problem is that over the years, CRM programs have advanced from simple, easy to use systems to complex behemoths that no one wants or understands. To prevent this, your CRM System should avoid the three basic mistakes in CRM design:

1. Tracking just current customers only works if you have 100% market share and you never again need to attract new customers. Since that is highly unlikely, you must also track your potential customers, however do not have a separate system for each. This just wastes time and energy, when in reality, the only reason for a CRM program is to ensure that your team is spending their sales resources on companies that are going to buy in the future, not just who has purchased in the past.

2. Don't just track who is going to buy, also track when. A CRM program that doesn't track this critical information is really just a glorified phone book! Your CRM program should include a mandatory field such as "Next Sales Contact Date". This will then change the filing method of your alphabetical phone book to a gold mine organized by the date of the prospects next purchase.

3. Every company that your organization ever contacts should be tracked, even if they may never buy from you. Not only it is important for your team to know where to go when, but it is also important for them to know where not to waste their time.

A Follow-Up File or CRM System ensures your sales representatives are in the right place at the right time, so they maximize their chances of making a sale. Some organizations understand the use of CRM Systems is so critical that they make using it a condition of employment for their sales representatives. Others take the time to explain that a CRM System is a critical sales tool that helps the sales representatives reach their goals, thus making them want to use it.

Regardless of whether the use of the system is your choice or theirs, administering it requires daily commitment from everyone. The system must be updated each and every day, no ifs, ands or buts! *Simply do not allow your sales representatives to leave the office until they have filed each and every call they made that day by the date of their next contact.* If their Follow-Up File requires for them to call a certain prospect today, then they should call today! Not only is it very impressive to a prospect when you do exactly what you said you were going to do, when you said you were going to do it, but it will also make them more likely to buy! This also goes a long way towards building reliability and trust with your customers.

Order Processing Training

In order to close a sale, your sales representative will need to complete the appropriate paperwork with their customers. As this function is part of the Presentation of Offer stage of the sales process, training on your order process should be included on your Sales Training Schedule.

It is a common misconception that sales people are not good at paperwork. In fact, the top sales producers, those making the highest incomes, most often produce the best paperwork. Why? They know that sloppy paperwork wastes time, is embarrassing in front of customers, and delays commission payments. Therefore, they simply choose to do it right the first time.

The paperwork needed to finalize a sale will depend on your product or service, as well as your company's order process. The last sheet in the *Presentation of Offer Planning Worksheet* workbook referenced earlier is the "Closing Interview Planning Worksheet". This is where you list all of the possible paperwork that a sales representative would require, what products they are used for, and if a customer signature is required.

Step 2 - Order Processing Paperwork		
List all the sales order processing paperwork required to sell your product or service in the chart below.		
Form Name	Required For What Products?	Customer Signature Required or For Internal Use Only

The idea of this workbook is to list every possible form, and where the sales representative would use it. In addition, you should also provide to your new sales people with copies of finalized orders where the paperwork is completed perfectly. Having this information on file so that your team can reference it later can make the whole order process system go more smoothly in the future.

Before you give this information to your sales representatives, it is also a good idea to have it checked by someone who is responsible to process your team's sales paperwork. Order processing is an area where a little teamwork between administration and sales can go a long way.

Here are some other guidelines for your sales representatives to follow to make your order process go smoother for all involved:

- Whenever possible, your sales representatives should have all the necessary sales paperwork completed before they arrive at the customer's location. This is much less stressful than trying to complete the paperwork when the prospect is watching.
- They should take the time and double check everything before hand. If they are not sure what they have done is correct, they should ask your order processing department before visiting the customer. An ounce of prevention is worth a pound of cure!
- They should always carry in their briefcase at least two blank copies of everything a customer may have to sign. If they make a mistake then they are with the customer, they will have a back up. This prevents having to put the sale on hold while they return to the office and then try and book another appointment to sign the new paperwork.

The next time you see a member of your sales team running out the door to sign an order, thinking that they do not have enough time to properly prepare for the closing meeting, get them to stop and think again. If they don't have time to do it right the first time, when are they going to find time to do it right the second time?

Company Procedure Training

Every company has procedures, with procedures being defined as your own particular way of doing things. They can be internal like how to claim expenses or book vacations, or they can be external like who delivers the product to the customer.

As policies and procedures vary widely from organization to organization, there is no way that your employees will know them before coming to work for you. You must discuss them with your new hires so that they have a thorough understanding of each and every procedure as it will pertain to them and their job as sales representatives.

It is best to create a list of all of the company procedures that your sales representatives will need to know. This list should include both internal and external procedures, as well as a clarification of roles and responsibilities.

Your list of internal procedures should include, but is not limited to the following:

- What are the expense account processes, what is allowed and who provides approvals
- What is the allowable vacation time, who must approve it, and how much advance notice is required
- How many sick days are allowed over what time frame, when is a documentation from a medical expert required, and how should a sick day be reported
- Does your company provide time off for bereavement, how much, and who is considered family
- If there are any health and safety regulations that must be adhered to, what are they, who is responsible for compliance, and how are violations reported
- Are there any formalized policies and procedures in place like ISO Standards, sales representative licensing requirements or union contracts that must be adhered to, what are they, and who is responsible for compliance

Depending on your product, your list of external procedures could include some or all of the following:

- After the sales order is complete, how long does it take for the customer to receive the product, and who delivers it
- Does your company require clarification on a pre-installation details such as having ample room for the equipment, proper electrical connections etc.
- Once the product has been delivered and is on site, who sets it up and when
- When set up is complete, who trains the customer, how long is the training program, and who pays for it
- Who does the customer call to reorder supplies, and what is the delivery turnaround
- How does an after sale service call get initiated, who completes the service work, and what are the wait times

Some of these procedures may have been included in your Human Resources Review, your Compensation Plan Review or your Order Processing training. Whatever was not covered there, needs to be discussed here. The key is to ensure your new hire knows all of the company procedures so that everyone is on the same page.

Performance Expectations & Monitoring

One of the biggest mistakes sales managers and their new hires make is that they fail to clearly define their shared performance expectations very early in the relationship. Not doing so is almost certain to cause misunderstandings in the future. To prevent this, you should make time to discuss with your new sales person what you expect from them, and what they expect from you as their sales manager.

Does the sale representative need to report to the office every day? Is attendance at sales meetings mandatory? How will the sales representative's sales performance be judged and what are the quotas? Is there a probationary period for new hires? What sales reports are required? Questions like these, if not discussed during the hiring process, should be clarified very early in the on-boarding process.

Once a new sales representative joins your sales team, you will want to ensure they all are on the right road to success. One of the most effective tools to monitor your team's performance is to require them to submit weekly sales reports like the *Activity Tracking Worksheet* and the *Sales Funnel Management Worksheet* shown below.

B B SALES CONNECTIONS — Activity Tracking Worksheet

Enter data in yellow boxes each week to calculate your sales process averages.

Your average commission rate	8.00%
Your average sale size	$ 10,000.00
The number of presentations it takes you to make a sale	3.00
The number of fact finds it takes you to make a presentation	2.00
The number of prospecting calls it takes you to book a fact find	15.00

Week Number	Number of Prospecting Calls Completed	Number of Fact Finds Completed	Number of Presentations Completed	Number of Sales Closed	Volume of Sales Closed	Commissions Earned
1	51	3	1	1	$ 12,000.00	$ 1,000.00
2	39	3	2	0	$ -	$ -
3	42	4	2	0	$ -	$ -
4	48	2	1	1	$ 8,000.00	$ 600.00
5						
6						

B B SALES CONNECTIONS — Sales Funnel Prospects

Enter data in yellow boxes each week to calculate your sales process averages. At the end of each month, delete all completed sales.

Company	Last Step of the Sales Process Completed?	Value of Potential Sale
ABC Company	Fact Find	$ 24,942.00
Profit Inc.	Presentation	$ 5,235.00
Super Sales Rep Corp.	Sale Completed	$ 7,565.00

Sales Funnel Management Worksheet

B2B SALES CONNECTIONS

Enter data in yellow boxes each week to calculate your sales process averages.

Your Monthly Sales Objective	$ 45,833.00
The number of presentations it takes you to make a sale	3.00
The number of fact finds it takes you to make a presentation	2.00

Sales Funnel Targets	Sales Process Step	Sales Funnel Actuals
$ 274,998.00	Fact Finds Completed	$ 302,945.00
$ 137,499.00	Presentations Completed	$ 153,940.00
$ 45,833.00	Sales Completed	$ 52,000.00

Some sales representatives, normally those who are not at quota, perceive sales reports as a policing action. "The boss is only checking up on me to ensure that I am doing my prospecting calls." Some have even been known to fudge the numbers just to avoid a confrontation. In reality, they are only hurting themselves.

The most successful sales representatives, look at sales reports differently. They see them as tools to monitor whether they are on course to reach their goals as identified earlier on their *Goal Setting & Action Planning Worksheet*. They also know that activity tracking can determine areas for improvement so they can be even more successful in the future, allowing them to work smarter, not harder.

Success Plan Checklist

Creating your 90 Day Sales Representative Success Plan takes a lot of thought and effort to produce. Some training schedules will overlap, and there are many tasks that must be completed. It is a lot of work when you are creating it however, the idea is you are creating a process that can be duplicated and reused whenever you need it. This process will actually save you time in the long run.

The *Success Plan Checklist* is a summary of all the tasks that must be completed when creating your Success Plan. It will ensure that your plan is completed and that you are pointing your sales team in right direction so you all can achieve your goals.

Yes, it is true, training sales representatives takes more time than it would to make the sales yourself. However, once your sales people become independent, training actually saves you time and allows the team to produce more sales overall.

SUCCESS PLAN CHECKLIST

Employee: _____

Department: _____

Employment Start Date: _____

Company Orientation

- Facility Tour
- Company Introduction Discussion
- Company Organization Chart Discussion
- 90 Day Success Plan Discussion

Human Resource Procedures

- Required Payroll Forms
- Distribution of Items on Basic Equipment List
- Asset Tracking Forms

Compensation Plan Review

- Compensation Plan Discussion
- Territory Assignment Discussion
- Compensation Plan Acknowledgement Form
- Personal Goal Definition Worksheet
- Goal Setting & Action Planning Worksheet

Product Training

- Product Knowledge Training Schedule Worksheet
- Implement Product Training Schedule With Trainee
- Competition Discussion
- Competition Website Listing

Sales Training

- Target Market Definition Worksheet
- Prospecting Approach Worksheet
- Fact Find Creation Worksheet
- Presentation of Offer Planning Worksheet
- Sales Training Schedule Worksheet
- Implement Sales Training Schedule With Trainee

CRM Systems Training

- Follow-up File or CRM System Creation
- CRM Training Included in Sales Training Schedule

Order Processing Training

- Sales Order Paperwork List
- Sample Orders
- Creation of Briefcase Paperwork File
- Order Processing Training Included in Sales Training

Company Procedures Training

- Internal Procedures List
- External Procedures List
- Company Procedures Discussion

Performance Expectation & Monitoring

- Shared Expectations Discussion
- Sales Report Discussion
- Activity Tracking Worksheet
- Sales Funnel Management Worksheet

CONCLUSION

Imagine once again that you are still in your rental car sitting in the airport parking lot and you still need to drive across town to a very important business meeting. The difference this time is that instead of having no help, you have every tool you need to make the trip, and you have a plan on how and when to use them. Now, not only can you make the trip successfully, you can make it faster and with less effort.

Your 90 Day Sales Representative Success Plan is just like having a map and a plan while sitting in the car at the airport. With it, not only will your sales team produce more sales, they will do so faster and with less effort. Yes, creating your plan is a lot of work, the first time, but in the long run the payoff will be worth it.

"Give a man a fish and you feed him for a day. Teach a man to fish and you feed him for a lifetime." – Chinese Proverb

APPENDIX – MANUAL CALCULATION FORMS

For those of you who are not familiar with Excel spreadsheets, all the calculations discussed in this training module can also be done manually. Simply print the forms on the following pages and follow the instructions.

Excel is a very common business software program. It is highly recommended that you take the time to learn the basics. Not only will you find that it can make your life much easier, you will find it to be a very profitable business tool as well.

ASSET TRACKING FORM

I acknowledge receipt of the following asset:

Asset Description: _____

Make: _____

Model: _____

Serial Number: _____

I understand that the use of this asset is for business purposes only.

I understand that this asset remains the property of _____.

I agree that this asset will be returned to the company upon request or termination of employment.

Employee: _____

Department: _____

Date: _____

Employee's Signature: _____

Manager's Signature: _____

COMPENSATION PLAN
ACKNOWLEDGEMENT FORM

I acknowledge that I have received and understand the contents of my Sales

Compensation Plan received from _____.

Employee: _____

Department: _____

Date: _____

Employee's Signature: _____

Manager's Signature: _____

Personal Goal Definition Worksheet

Step 1 - Personal Commitment	
I am committed to and will work towards achieving my personal goals as listed below.	
Name	
Date	

Step 2 - Lifestyle & Leisure Time Goals	
Next 12 Months	
Next 2 - 4 Years	
Long Term	

Step 3 - Career & Educational Goals	
Next 12 Months	
Next 2 - 4 Years	
Long Term	

Step 4 - Health & Fitness Goals	
Next 12 Months	
Next 2 - 4 Years	
Long Term	

Step 5 - Spirtual & Community Involvement Goals	
Next 12 Months	
Next 2 - 4 Years	
Long Term	

Step 6 - Financial Goals	
Next 12 Months	
Next 2 - 4 Years	
Long Term	

Step 7 - Annual Income Goal	
To fund my desired lifestyle and achieve my goals as outlined above, I must earn an annual income of	
Signature	

Goal Setting & Action Planning Worksheet

1. What is the total annual income you wish to earn to fund your lifestyle?
2. What is your base salary?
3. What is your average monthly bonus earned?
4. Amount of commission income required to reach annual income goal. (#1-(#2 + #3))
5. What is your average commission rate?
6. Total annual sales volume required. ((#4 / #5) x 100)
7. Monthly sales volume required. (#6 / 12)
8. What is you average size of sale?
9. Total number of sales required per month. (#7 / #8)
10. Total number of sales required per week. (#9 / 4)
11. How many presentations does it take you to make a sale?
12. Number of presentations required per month. (#9 x #11)
13. Number of presentations required per week. (#12 / 4)
14. How many fact finds does it take you to make a presentation?
15. Number of fact finds required per month. (#13 x #14)
16. Number of fact finds required per week. (#15 / 4)
17. How many prospecting calls does it take you to book a fact find?
18. Number of prospecting calls required per month. (#15 x #17)
19. Number of prospecting calls required per week. (#18 / 4)
20. Number of prospecting calls required per day. (#19 / 5)

Product Listing
Worksheet

Number	Product Training Topics	Available Trainers	Available Training Methods
1			
2			
3			
4			
5			
6			
7			
8			
9			
10			
11			
12			

Product Training Schedule Worksheet

Trainee				Product Training or Employment Start Date		
Week Number	Product	Trainer	Training Method	Training Starts Week Of	Complete?	Notes

B2B SALES CONNECTIONS

Target Market Characteristic Definitions

Number	Type of Business Listing	Number of Employees Listing	Annual Revenue Listing	Product Category Purchased Listing	Product Usage Listing	Previous Supplier Listing	Related Product Listing	Other Commonality Listing #1	Other Commonality Listing #2
1									
2									
3									
4									
5									
6									
7									
8									
9									
10									
11									
12									
13									
14									
15									
16									
17									
18									
19									
20									
21									
22									
23									
24									
25									
26									
27									
28									
29									
30									
31									
32									
33									
34									
35									
36									
37									
38									
39									
40									
41									
42									
43									
44									
45									
46									
47									
48									
49									
50									

B B SALES CONNECTIONS

Target Market Definition Worksheet

Customer Name	Volume of Sale	Type of Business	Number of Employees	Annual Revenue	Product Category Purchased	Product Usage	Previous Supplier	Related Product	Other Commonality #1	Other Commonality #2

SALES
CONNECTIONS

**Target Market Definition
Analysis**

Class Of Characteristic	Characteristic	Customer Count	Sales Volume	Customer Count Percentage	Sales Volume Percentage
	Totals				

Prospecting Approach
Worksheet

Step 1 - Opening Statement	
Hi, I hope you can help me. I am looking for the name of the person in charge of	

Step 2 - Headline				
Hi, my name is		of		company.
We've been able to help companies similar to yours				

Step 3 - Qualifying Questions	
Qualifing Question #1	
Qualifing Question #2	
Qualifing Question #3	
Qualifing Question #4	
Qualifing Question #5	
Time Frame Question #1	
Time Frame Question #2	

Step 4 - Agreement to Move To Next Step Statement			
Based on the information that you have provided, I believe that I can help you			
The next step is			
Are you available on		or do you prefer	
Thank you very much for your time.			

**Fact Find Creation
Worksheet**

Step 1 - Opening Greeting	
As I mentionned to you on the phone, I believe the use of our	
could help you	
Before I can tell you more about how I may be able to do that, I need to learn more about you and your company.	
To make the best use of our time, I have prepared a number of questions that will help us uncover the information that I need. May I proceed?	

Step 2 - General Company Questions	
Question #1	
Question #2	
Question #3	
Question #4	
Question #5	

Step 3 - Product & Industry Specific Questions	
Potential Want #1	
Questions	
Potential Want #2	
Questions	
Potential Want #3	
Questions	
Potential Want #4	
Questions	
Potential Want #5	
Questions	
Potential Want #6	
Questions	

Step 4 - Financial & Buying Process Questions	
Question #1	
Question #2	
Question #3	
Question #4	
Question #5	

Step 5 - Agreement to Move To Next Step Statement		
Based on the information that you have provided, I believe that I can help you		
The next step is		
Are you available on	or do you prefer	
Thank you very much for your time.		

Written Proposal Template Creation
Worksheet

Step 1 - Title Page					
Does your template title page include the following headings? Answer "Y" or "N".				Date:	
Proposal For:		Prepared For:	Presented By:	Subject:	
Subject Statement					

Step 2 - Company Information
What company information will you include in your template?

Step 3 - Present Situation Assessment
Using the questions created on the Fact Find Creation Worksheet in Section 2, create Present Situation statements.
Statement 1
Statement 2
Statement 3
Statement 4
Statement 5

Step 4 - Proposed Solution
Using the Presentation Situation statements created above, create Proposed Solution statements.
Statement 1
Statement 2
Statement 3
Statement 4
Statement 5

Step 5 - Financial Considerations					
Should your template include the following Financial Considerations? Answer "Y" or "N".				Purchase Price	
Financing Options		Cost Comparison	ROI Analysis	Terms & Conditions	
List of Terms & Conditions					

Step 6 - Implementation Schedule & Shared Expectations
List all of your required sales order paperwork.
List your order processing, delivery & installation time frames and schedules.

Demonstration Planning Worksheet

Step 1 - Products To Be Demonstrated	
List all products to be demonstrated.	

Step 2 - Site Preparation	
Have the products to be demonstrated been set up and tested?	
Have you rehearsed the demonstration?	
How long is the demonstration?	
Are the supplies and materials needed for the demonstration available?	
Is there a white board in the room?	
Is the demonstration room neat and tidy?	

Step 3 - Customer Issues	
List the 3 biggest issues the customer is experiencing, and outline how they will be solved by the demonstrated products.	
Problem 1	
Problem 2	
Problem 3	

Step 1 - Objection Preparation
List 5 common true objections that you may receive and outline possible solutions.

Objection 1	
Objection 2	
Objection 3	
Objection 4	
Objection 5	

Step 2 - Order Processing Paperwork

List all the sales order processing paperwork required to sell your product or service in the chart below.

Form Name	Required For What Products?	Customer Signature Required or For Internal Use Only

**After Sale Follow-Up Planning
Worksheet**

Step 1 - Satisfied Customer Script					
Mr. Customer, it has been about		since we			
In your opinion, do you feel we have accomplished what we set out to do?					
Are you satisfied with our products and services?		What is it that you are most satisfied with?			
May I use you as a reference for other potential customers?					
Would it be possible for you to put your comments into a refrence letter for me?					

Step 2 - Product Reordering Procedures & Company Contacts

Mr. Customer, here is a list of other important contacts and procedures to ensue that you remain a happy customer.

Contact	Reason for Contact	Method of Contact

Step 3 - Related Products Script

Mr. Customer, while implmenting this project, I noticed that you are experiencing		
Many of our customers similar to you who use	have told us that our	
has also		
I would like to investigate this further with you. Are you available on	or do you prefer	

Step 4 - Referral Request Script

Mr. Customer, you have stated that you are very happy with the benefits that you have received from our	
Are there any other companies that you know of that I should be contacting so that they can realize those same benefits?	
Who should I contact?	
May I tell tham that I was recommended by you?	Thank you.

Sales Function Listing
Worksheet

Number	Sales Training Topics	Available Trainers	Available Training Methods
1			
2			
3			
4			
5			
6			
7			
8			
9			
10			
11			
12			

Sales Training Schedule Worksheet

Trainee				Sales Training or Employment Start Date		

Week Number	Sales Function	Trainer	Training Method	Training Starts Week Of	Complete?	Notes

Activity Tracking Worksheet

Your average commission rate (Total Commissions Earned / Total Volume of Sales Closed)

Your average size sale (Total Volume of Sales Closed / Total Number of Sales Closed)

The number of presentations it takes you to make a sale (Total Number of Presentations / Total number of Sales Closed)

The number of fact finds it takes you to make a presentation (Total Number of Fact Finds / Total Number of Presentations)

The number of prospecting calls it takes you to book a fact find (Total Number of Prospecting Calls / Total number of Fact Finds)

Week Number	Number of Prospecting Calls Completed	Number of Fact Finds Completed	Number of Presentations Completed	Number of Sales Closed	Volume of Sales Closed	Commissions Earned
1						
2						
3						
4						
5						
6						
7						
8						
9						
10						
11						
12						
13						
14						
15						
16						
17						
18						
19						
20						
21						
22						
23						
24						
25						
26						
27						
28						
29						
30						
31						
32						
33						
34						
35						
36						
37						
38						
39						
40						
41						
42						
43						
44						
45						
46						
47						
48						
49						
50						
51						
52						
Totals						

Sales Funnel
Prospects

Company	Last Step of the Sales Process Completed?	Value of Potential Sale

Sales Funnel Management Worksheet

Your Monthly Sales Objective

The number of presentations it takes you to make a sale

The number of fact finds it takes you to make a presentation

Sales Funnel Targets	Sales Process Step	Sales Funnel Actuals
$ - (Your Monthly Value for Presentations Below X The Number of Fact Finds to Make a Presentation)	Fact Finds Completed	$ - (The Total of Fact Finds Completed from Sales Funnel Prospects Form)
$ - (Your Monthly Sales Objective X The Number of Presentations to Make a Sale)	Presentations Completed	$ - (The Total of Presentations Completed from Sales Funnel Prospects Form)
$ - (Your Monthy Sales Objective)	Sales Completed	$ - (The Total of Sales Completed from Sales Funnel Prospects Form)

SUCCESS PLAN CHECKLIST

Employee: _____

Department: _____

Employment Start Date: _____

Company Orientation

Completed

- Facility Tour ☐
- Company Introduction Discussion ☐
- Company Organization Chart Discussion ☐
- 90 Day Success Plan Discussion ☐

Human Resource Procedures

- Required Payroll Forms ☐
- Distribution of Items on Basic Equipment List ☐
- Asset Tracking Forms ☐

Compensation Plan Review

- Compensation Plan Discussion ☐
- Territory Assignment Discussion ☐
- Compensation Plan Acknowledgement Form ☐
- Personal Goal Definition Worksheet ☐
- Goal Setting & Action Planning Worksheet ☐

Product Training

- Product Knowledge Training Schedule Worksheet ☐
- Implement Product Training Schedule With Trainee ☐
- Competition Discussion ☐
- Competition Website Listing ☐

Sales Training   Completed

- Target Market Definition Worksheet   ☐
- Prospecting Approach Worksheet   ☐
- Fact Find Creation Worksheet   ☐
- Presentation of Offer Planning Worksheet   ☐
- Sales Training Schedule Worksheet   ☐
- Implement Sales Training Schedule With Trainee   ☐

CRM Systems Training

- Follow-up File or CRM System Creation   ☐
- CRM Training Included in Sales Training Schedule   ☐

Order Processing Training

- Sales Order Paperwork List   ☐
- Sample Orders   ☐
- Creation of Briefcase Paperwork File   ☐
- Order Processing Training Included in Sales Training Schedule   ☐

Company Procedures Training

- Internal Procedures List   ☐
- External Procedures List   ☐
- Company Procedures Discussion   ☐

Performance Expectation & Monitoring

- Shared Expectations Discussion   ☐
- Sales Report Discussion   ☐
- Activity Tracking Worksheet   ☐
- Sales Funnel Management Worksheet   ☐

Chapter 4 – You Are The Coach! Ongoing Management Tools

"The signs of a good sales manager
are teeth marks on his tongue." –
Author Unknown

YOU ARE THE COACH!

If you were to look up the meaning of a coach in a dictionary, you will probably find definitions like "the person who is in overall charge of a team and its strategy" or "one who instructs or trains a team of performers". Sound familiar? Of course it does. One could use the exact same words to describe a sales manager.

Just like the great sports coaches Scottie Bowman and Lou Holtz discussed earlier in this training course, you are the coach of your team! You must teach what needs to be taught, you must lead where they need to be led, and you must motivate so they follow you there. The sales force may drive your company's revenue, but it is your job as sales manager to drive the sales force!

Like all great coaches, you don't actually play the game, you teach others how to play it. Your job is not to sell for your sales representatives, rather it is to teach them how to sell. Sure, you could do it yourself. Many unsuccessful sales managers have tried. But wouldn't it be better to have ten others just like you selling instead?

The best sales managers know their primary responsibility is to develop their people, not themselves. Would Scotty Bowman strap on a pair of skates with 30 seconds left in the third period of the Stanley Cup Final? Of course not, and neither should you.

Sometimes it may appear to be faster and easier to do the task yourself rather than train your people to do it. True, it might be quicker for you the first time, but what about when it needs to be the second, third of fourth times? Do you really want to service that open sales territory or fix a sales representative's sloppy paperwork? If you never hire or train someone else to do it, you will always have to do it yourself. Do you run your business or does your business run you?

Sometimes, despite your best intentions, you still have to complete a task yourself because only you are the only one with the proper knowledge and skill to do so. This could happen in a high end sales call or a difficult customer service situation. When this happens, look at these situations as opportunities to train someone else to do it while you are completing the task. Once someone sees you do something often enough, eventually they will not need you to do it for them anymore. In the long run, you will save time and be more productive if you "show how, not do for". Even when the pressure is on, always stop and think if the task at hand is also a training opportunity to develop someone on your team.

How do you know if you are on the right track in developing your team? Most would say that the best test of a sales manager's coaching ability is what happens if you are no longer there. For example, think back to your first day at work after your last vacation. Did you return to the office to find that everything came to a grinding halt while you are away, or did they barely miss you while you were gone?

Always ask yourself, if you were to leave the organization tomorrow, could your sales team carry on and still produce at the sales level they are now? If the answer is yes, then you are definitely moving in the right direction. If the answer is no, then you must start to develop your team using effective sales management tools. If you can't even remember when you were able to take your last vacation, then you should start the training process today. After all, if you want to move onto bigger and better things, you must train your replacement first.

ONGOING SALES MANAGEMENT TOOLS

You are in charge of properly managing the day to day operations of your sales team so they produce the required results today and in the future. To accomplish this, there are many ongoing sales management tools used by successful managers. They include:

- Group sales meetings
- One on one coaching meetings
- Joint field work
- Testing
- Activity reporting and forecasting tools
- Performance reviews
- Sales incentive contests

When used correctly, these sales management tools can develop a sales team and take them to heights only limited by their own imaginations.

Group Sales Meetings

Group sales meetings are one of the most common tools used by sales managers to train and motivate their sales teams. Although most sales managers hold regular meetings, few actually conduct productive sales meetings, and unfortunately, most just end up being a waste of valuable sales time.

Your sales meetings should be held at the same time each week, and for the same duration, so that your team can plan their sales appointments accordingly. For example, Monday morning meetings held between 8:30 am and 9:30 am are a great way to start your team's week off on the right foot.

It is advisable to make attendance at your sales meetings mandatory for your entire sales team. If you have out of town sales representatives where travel to the meeting is an issue, they should join the meeting via a conference call or web connection. If you have written materials or presentation files, you could email them in advance so those on the phone can easily follow the meeting. Not only will that ensure that everyone is receiving the same message, but the out of town sales representatives will feel that they are more a part of the team as well.

Make sure you always start on time, no matter what. Nothing rewards tardy behavior more than making those who showed up on time wait for those who are late. When 8:30 am rolls around, just shut the door and start the meeting. You will only have to do this once or twice before your entire team will be in the board room at 8:25 waiting for you to start the meeting.

Obviously, this requires that you make the personal commitment to be on time as well. If your entire team is left waiting for you to start the meeting, it only reinforces that being late is acceptable behavior. It also shows your team that you don't respect their time. No matter what, always be on time for your own meeting.

Not only must you start your meetings on time, you must also finish on time. You need to follow your own time commitment so your team can get on with the rest of their sales day as planned. It is better to do what you say you are going to do by delaying a discussion topic for a week, than to have your sales team racing in traffic because you made them late for their first sales appointment.

How long should your sales meetings last? Special meetings like new product launches can be a full day or more, but regularly schedules sales meetings should last no longer than an hour. Any longer and your attendees will start to lose interest. You could talk longer, but what you are saying won't really be sinking in, so why bother waste your time and that of your sales team. It is better to have shorter weekly meetings than it is to have one long and drawn out monthly meeting.

In order to fit everything that needs to be discussed in just an hour, an effective sales meeting needs preparation. You should have a predetermined agenda so that the meeting stays on schedule, with preplanned discussion topics that create value to the sales representatives who attend.

Start your sales meeting by discussing sales results for the entire group, and then take the time to publicly recognize your best performers. Psychology studies show that sales people work as hard for peer recognition as they do for their commission, so be sure not to skip this step. This also sets a very upbeat tone for the rest of the meeting.

On the reverse, don't criticize a team member for poor sales results in the meeting. This serves no purpose other than to create a negative environment for the whole team. You need to keep the meeting positive and motivating. Derogatory comments from you or from a sales representative can create a negative attitude that can spread through your sales team like a cancer spreads through a healthy body. It is better to not say anything at all, or to take the negative into a one on one meeting afterward, than it is to discuss it in a group sales meeting.

After you clear up any general announcements, you should move into the team development section of the meeting. This could include sales tips, product knowledge facts, role plays, product demonstrations, guest speakers or creating a training session based on common questions from your sales representatives.

As a general rule of thumb, if you receive the same question from two different sales people in a short period of time, it is an excellent topic for a sales meeting. It's not that the others on your team don't want to ask the same question, they just haven't gotten around to it yet. Answer a question individually, and you will have to answer it several times, but answer it in a sales meeting, and you answer it only once.

For ideas on specific discussion topics, you could keep a file folder labeled "Sales Meeting Ideas". As discussion topics pop up during the week, just place a reminder note into the file. On the Friday before the meeting when you are preparing your agenda, review your file and choose a theme for Monday's meeting. For example, if a new order process procedure is resulting in a number of questions from the sales people, you could write a note for your file to remind you to arrange for someone from the Order Processing Department to speak at your meeting. Or if you read a newsletter with a great sales lesson, put it in your folder so that you share it with your team.

Next, you may want to have your each of your representatives give a very short sales forecast for the upcoming week. The key is to keep it really short with just the names of the companies to close and the dollar amounts. This is not a one on one meeting taking place in front of a group. That just wastes the time of those sales people who have to sit there and just listen while another speaks. If you want specific individual forecast updates, then meet individually with your sales representatives.

After a short question and answer period, you will want to end the meeting on a high note. Perhaps your sales representatives could share their best sales success of the past week, or you could end with a motivational quote or story that ties the whole meeting together. Remember, this is the last thing your team will hear before heading out the door, so keep it positive.

On the next page is an example of a sales meeting agenda. It was created using the Excel spreadsheet, *Sales Meeting Agenda Worksheet.xls*. The workbook allows you to plan a sales meeting with up to 20 agenda items of various durations, resulting in the total meeting length duration at the bottom. When you click on a cell to enter the start time of the meeting and the duration of each item, a drop down arrow will appear. You simply click on your selection to enter the information.

	Microsoft Excel - Workbook 1 - Sales Meeting Agenda Worksheet.xls

File Edit View Insert Format Tools Data Window Help Adobe PDF

C44   *fx* 12:05:00 AM

	A	B	C	D	E
1	**SALES CONNECTIONS**				**Sales Meeting Agenda Worksheet**
2					
3			**Enter data in the yellow boxes to create your Sales Meeting Agenda**		
4					
5	Title	Weekly Sales Meeting			
6	Purpose	Eliminate Order Processing Errors On New Contracts to Save Time for Sales Department			
7	Date	Monday, July 20, 2009			
8					
36					
37	**Start Time**	**End Time**	**Duration**	**Presenter**	**Discussion Topic**
38	8:30 AM	8:35 AM	0:05	Mathew Manager	Group Sales Results
39	8:35 AM	8:40 AM	0:05	Mathew Manager	Public Recognition for Quota Busters
40	8:40 AM	8:45 AM	0:05	Mathew Manager	Announcements
41	8:45 AM	9:10 AM	0:25	Peter Processor	Order Processing Training
42	9:10 AM	9:20 AM	0:10	Team	Individual Rep Forecasts & Sales Success Stories
43	9:20 AM	9:25 AM	0:05	Team	Questions & Answers
44	9:25 AM	9:30 AM	0:05	Mathew Manager	Closing with Motivational Quote
45	9:30 AM		0:05		
46			0:10		
47			0:15		
48			0:20		
49			0:25		
50			0:30		
51			0:35		
52			0:40		
53					
54					
55					
56					
57					
58	**Total**		1:00		
59					

Sheet1 / Sheet2 / Sheet3 /

Ready

For those of you not familiar with Excel, you can plan your sales meeting agenda by using the form found in Appendix A.

One On One Meetings

A one on one meeting is a management tool commonly used by sales managers to connect and relate with their sales representatives as individuals. Sometimes it is best to discuss personal issues privately, as opposed to sharing them publicly in a group sales meeting.

You should hold a one on one meeting with each member of your team once a month at the very least. Some managers have found that shorter weekly meetings work better than longer monthly meetings. If a sales representative is new to selling your product, or if they are not performing well in relation to their objectives, you may need to hold your meetings more frequently. How often you meet will depend on your own specific situation however, it is better to meet too often than to not communicate enough. You don't want to over-manage your people, but you don't want to leave them to flounder either.

Regardless of the frequency, time spent in meetings takes away from time spent selling. You must plan your meetings ahead to time so that they are productive for both you and the sales representative. As such, a weekly meeting should last no longer than 30 minutes, and a monthly meeting, no longer than an hour.

Time spent traveling to and from the office for the meeting is not productive. If travel time is an issue, your meeting could also be scheduled with an out of town sales representative by telephone. You should conduct this meeting the same way you would if it was a face to face meeting in your office. Regardless of the distance, you should strive for at least one face to face meeting with every sales representative at least once per quarter.

You always want to stay positive in a one on one meeting, however if issues or problems exist, this is the time to discuss them. A sales representative not only needs to know what is working well, but also the areas for improvement, and the action plan and timing to fix them.

You should also keep a file or binder for each sales representative that includes all of their previous sales reports and meeting notes so that you can monitor their progress over time. This file will be crucial if you need to take disciplinary actions in the future. Proper documentation can protect you from litigation in the future.

The agenda for your one on one meeting should focus on the following three areas:

1. Sales activities and results since the last meeting
2. Sales activities and forecasts to occur before the next meeting
3. Action items to be completed before the next meeting

Sales activities and results since the last meeting will be recorded on the reports that your team will submit to you. The specific forms *Activity Tracking Worksheet, Sales Funnel Prospects,* and *Sales Funnel Management Worksheets* were discussed in Section 3 of this training course and will also be reviewed again later. When you review these reports with your sales representative as opposed to just reading them on your own, you gain a much better understanding of the sales activities completed. You will also know what stage of the sales process was completed for each prospect contacted, and the current status of the sales funnel.

Notice that reviewing sales reports only looks at what has already occurred. It is important to look ahead at what is going to be done, as opposed to just looking at what was previously completed. You can't change the past. You can't go back to last week and tell your sales representative to do more sales calls. You can however, learn from the past so that you can make the necessary changes to have a better future.

The last two items on your one on one meeting agenda deal with the future, and are discussed using the *One on One Meeting Planner Worksheet* shown on the next page.

The first section outlines the sales which are expected to close, what steps the sales representative will take to move the sale forward, and how he plans to complete it. When you review the sales forecast and compare it to previous forecasts you have kept on file, take note of how many times you have seen the same sale forecasted to close.

If the same sale is always forecasted meeting after meeting, ask the sales representative what specifically is going to change this month to make it close. If you do not get a very specific answer, chances are you will see the same account forecasted again next meeting. The main objective of this part of the meeting is for you both to get an accurate estimate of sales that will close, not sales they only wish would close.

The second part of the Meeting Planner also focuses on what will happen in the future. It examines prospects that are further up the sales funnel, and concentrates on what is going to be done to move them through. Again, this discussion should speak to specifics, with every contact with a prospect having a detailed purpose. For example, just telephoning a prospect that popped up in this month's follow up file won't do anything to move a prospect forward, however, phoning to clarify the outstanding questions about product specifications will. You don't want professional visitors who just call to say hello, you want professional sales people who are taking action to move the sale forward.

One on One Meeting Planner

SALES CONNECTIONS

Enter information in the yellow boxes to create your One on One Meeting Planner

Sales Representative	Sam Sales Representative
Date	Monday, July 20, 2009
Date of Next Meeting	Monday, July 27, 2009

Expected Sales To Close Before Next Meeting

Company	Plan of Action	Purpose of Call
ABC Company	Face to face meeting	Pick up signed contracts
123 Profit Inc	Phone call	Follow up on customer faxing contracts

Follow-up On Hot Prospects Before Next Meeting

Company	Plan of Action	Purpose of Call
Hoho Corp.	Face to face meeting	Present proposal
Superstar Synergies	Face to face meeting	Fact find meeting
Wow Inc.	Phone call	Follow Up on Board Meeting results

Action Items to Be Completed Before The Next Meeting

Action Item	Plan of Action	To Be Completed By
Improve Widget product knowledge	Read instruction manual	Sam Sales Representative
Complainer Inc is unhappy customer	Phone call	Mathew Manager

Other Objectives, Comments, and To-Do's

Sam is having an outstanding year. The key is to ensure that he continues to prospect so that those results continue.

Finally, the Meeting Planner lists the action items that need to be discussed, and who is responsible for their completion. Many different topics could be listed including customer service issues, order processing procedures, day to day operations, training requirements, sales performance, and personal concerns. Literally anything that needs to be put on the table and discussed should be listed.

This section is essentially a to-do list that must be completed before the next meeting for both you and your representative. For example, if you meet weekly, then only the tasks that must be completed in the upcoming week should be listed. If a project is larger and needs more time to complete, then just list the tasks within the project that must be completed before the next meeting. For example, to improve product knowledge, perhaps one Meeting Planner item would list reading the brochure, the next week's planner lists reading the operator's manual, and then the next lists hands on product training.

A one on one meeting is your opportunity to connect and relate with your sales representatives as individuals. Only proper planning and preparation on your part will make this tool effective. Otherwise, your meeting will only be seen as time that could have been better spent selling.

Also, don't underestimate the importance of your sales representatives' need to have the opportunity to make a connection with you in a one on one meeting. Your sales people are your customers, with your top performers being your best ones. As the old saying goes, if you don't take care of your customers, someone else will.

Joint Field Work

Joint field work is where you and your representative make sales calls together. They could be telemarketing calls from the office, or meetings with customers. The sales representatives will benefit and learn from your knowledge and experience, yet they are still are not working without a net, so to speak.

The problem most sales managers have when doing joint field work is they end up taking over the call completely. Some even forget the sales person is in the room! The key is not to "do for", it is to "show how". Taking over a sales call does nothing to train or develop the sales representative. The real purpose of doing joint field work today is so your sales representative won't need you on sales calls in the future.

Like everything else, development of your sales team through the use of joint field work needs to be planned in advance. You must ensure that each session is moving the sales representative forward towards being an independent and productive sales professional.

You must identify the skills they need to develop, and then you must follow a proven process so that they can learn them.

More specifically, developing a skill in a sales representative through joint field work is a five step process:

1. Skill Identification – You first must identify the skill that you need to develop in your sales representative. Examples include telephone prospecting, fact finding, live demonstrations etc.

2. Training Stage – You need to teach the skill, its purpose, and how to perform it properly. This may require multiple training sessions to complete.

3. Sales Rep Observation Stage– This is where the sales representative watches you perform the skill with customers in the field. Essentially, you are showing them how to do it. Again this may require more than one session to complete.

4. Manager Observation Stage – Once they have seen the skill performed often enough, it's time for them to try it for themselves. In this stage, the sales representative starts to practice the skill while you observe. For example, you may listen while they do prospecting calls on the phone, or join them on a call when they present a proposal to a customer. At this stage, you must provide feedback by reinforcing the right behavior and correcting the wrong behavior. After several joint calls, this feedback will allow the sales representative to hone their skill until they become independent.

5. Coaching Stage – Once you have observed the sales representative's ability to perform the skill properly, you must motivate and coach them to use it repeatedly. Development is not complete until proper use of the skill is an internalized habit that is performed unconsciously. Again, this stage occurs over several calls and sometimes over an extended period of time. In fact, some managers say the coaching stage never really ends!

The *Joint Field Work Planner* shown on the next page is a worksheet that will help you plan and track your joint field work with your sales representative through the five steps mentioned above. A copy of this planner should be kept in the representative's activity file or binder discussed earlier so that it can be reviewed with the sales person at your one on one meetings.

B2B SALES CONNECTIONS

Joint Field Work Planner

Enter information in the yellow boxes to create your Joint Field Work Planner

Sales Representative	Sam Sales Representative
Manager	Mathew Manager

Skill To Be Developed	Training Session Complete?					Sales Rep Observes Manager Complete?					Manager Observes Sales Rep Complete?						Coaching Stage			
Telephone Prosecting	X	X	X			X	X				X	X	X	X	X	X				
Fact Finding	X	X	X			X	X	X			X									

As stated earlier, developing a skill could require a number of joint sales calls at each stage for a sales representative to master just one skill. Also, several skills could be in development at the same time. As such, it is important to track what has been done on your Joint Field Work Planner so that you ensure that you are developing all the required skills in your sales representative, and that you are using your valuable joint field work time wisely.

Where ever possible, you should schedule joint field work with each member of your team at least once per quarter, regardless of their experience or skill level. It is always a good idea to observe your representatives in the field to ensure they stay sharp, and continue to practice the skills that made them successful in the first place.

Before going on a joint call with your representative, always ensure that you both have a clear understanding of the purpose of the call before hand. You should also discuss what role you are going to play in the interaction. For example, the sales representative may ask the operational questions in a fact find interview, yet will need your assistance with the financial questions. When you both know what you want to accomplish, you have a greater chance of working together to achieve it. More importantly, it will be less likely that you will just take over the appointment, therefore losing the opportunity for the sales representative to learn from the experience.

Remember, the goal is to push the baby bird out of the nest, so to speak. However, he will never be able to take his first solo flight if he is only allowed to fly on your back. In other words, when you are observing your sales representative in an appointment, bite your tongue and observe! Don't take over an appointment too early. Only jump in if they ask you for your assistance or if they really are really stumbling.

As soon after the appointment as possible, while everything is still fresh in your mind, you will want to discuss the call with your sales person. In the elevator, riding down with the prospect's assistant is too early, but in the car still parked in the customer's parking lot where you can speak privately is not. You have to tell the representative what needs to improve in the next appointment, but you also must tell them what they did right as well.

Begin by asking what he thinks went well and what he thinks needs improvement, as opposed to you just telling him your opinion. Sales people tend to think they performed worse in the appointment than they actually did. Also, they were probably nervous working with their boss. Once they have provided their analysis of the call, you should then talk about what you saw as working well, and what could be improved for future appointments.

Always end on a positive note. Sales people can get down on themselves pretty quickly, and that serves no purpose to anyone. You want your representative leaving the joint field work session feeling good about the experience and secure in the knowledge that you want them to succeed. If you lost a sale, help them to learn from it, and move on. If you closed a sale together, give them all the credit and recognition for it, especially in front of other members of the sales team. As sales manager, you take all of the crap, but none of the glory.

Testing

What is one way to check if your child is sick? You could stick a thermometer in their mouth and take their temperature. By doing so, you see a clear picture of where their health stands at the moment you receive the reading. Think of a test given to your sales representatives as your thermometer. Once given, you see a snapshot of where their sales skill health stands at a particular moment in time.

The best sales managers rely heavily on the information they receive from testing to quickly see what is working and what needs improvement. Not only is it a great temperature gauge for the skill levels of their representatives, but also for their own teaching and coaching skills. There is no better way to see if the methods you are using to develop your sales people are working by having them prove it on a test.

There are many quick and easy ways to take the temperature of your sales team:

- For new hires, finish each section of the Sales and Product Training sessions as described in your 90 Day Success Play with a written exam. For example, you could have an exam for each step of the sales process, including prospecting, fact finding and presenting. Present the representative with a written diploma once he or she successfully completes all the exams, and display it in a public place. Not only does this build pride and confidence in your sales representative, but it also builds credibility with customers and other employees in the company to see that all your sales team is trained and certified.

- After every training session with your team, have the representatives complete a quick one page quiz. You will even find that they are more attentive during the training session when they know there is a test at the end. The questions should focus on what you wanted them to learn in the session. Even if some of the questions asked were answered incorrectly, you will gain another teaching opportunity when you go over the right answers with the group. This repetition of the material will increase their retention of the topic as well.

- To test sales skills, have the representatives perform role plays in front of others. For example, you could have your representative perform a sample product demonstration at a sales meeting, or they could role play a fact find with someone in your company. The feedback you receive serves as an excellent temperature reading of the skill performed.

- Games can also serve as excellent tests of skill. You could be very creative with trivia games based on product knowledge specifications, or timed trials on certain demonstration skills. For example, one sales manager had great success in a meeting by playing her own version of the popular TV game show, Jeopardy. The dollar value of one square was earned by successfully answering a product knowledge question from different categories, with the winning sales representative earning a small gift certificate as a prize. Other managers have had success with their own versions of bingo, Trivial Pursuit ™, or Match Game™. You are only limited by your own imagination!

To improve your effectiveness as a sales manager, incorporate some form of testing into your management style. After all, if you don't keep score, how are you going to know if you are winning?

Activity Reporting & Forecasting Tools

The concept of monitoring a sales representative's performance was first introduced in Section 3 of this training course. As discussed, the worksheets *Activity Tracking Worksheet, Sales Funnel Prospects,* and *Sales Funnel Management Worksheets* shown below should be submitted to you weekly by each member of your sales team. You should then discuss these reports with the representative in your one on one meeting.

Activity Tracking Worksheet

B B SALES CONNECTIONS

Enter data in yellow boxes each week to calculate your sales process averages.

Your average commission rate	8.00%
Your average sale size	$ 10,000.00
The number of presentations it takes you to make a sale	3.00
The number of fact finds it takes you to make a presentation	2.00
The number of prospecting calls it takes you to book a fact find	15.00

Week Number	Number of Prospecting Calls Completed	Number of Fact Finds Completed	Number of Presentations Completed	Number of Sales Closed	Volume of Sales Closed	Commissions Earned
1	51	3	1	1	$ 12,000.00	$ 1,000.00
2	39	3	2	0	$ -	$ -
3	42	4	2	0	$ -	$ -
4	48	2	1	1	$ 8,000.00	$ 600.00
5						
6						

Sales Funnel Prospects

B B SALES CONNECTIONS

Enter data in yellow boxes each week to calculate your sales process averages. At the end of each month, delete all completed sales.

Company	Last Step of the Sales Process Completed?	Value of Potential Sale
ABC Company	Fact Find	$ 24,942.00
Profit Inc.	Presentation	$ 5,235.00
Super Sales Rep Corp.	Sale Completed	$ 7,565.00

Sales Funnel Management Worksheet

B B SALES CONNECTIONS

Enter data in yellow boxes each week to calculate your sales process averages.

Your Monthly Sales Objective	$ 45,833.00
The number of presentations it takes you to make a sale	3.00
The number of fact finds it takes you to make a presentation	2.00

Sales Funnel Targets	Sales Process Step	Sales Funnel Actuals
$ 274,998.00	Fact Finds Completed	$ 302,945.00
$ 137,499.00	Presentations Completed	$ 153,940.00
$ 45,833.00	Sales Completed	$ 52,000.00

In most circumstances, these sales reports, coupled with the forecasting section on the *One on One Meeting Planner* discussed earlier and shown again below, are all that you should need from your sales representatives. These tools should allow you to manage the day to day sales activities of your team, while still produce accurate forecasts. If a sales representative is consistently working hard, providing accurate forecasts, and more importantly producing sales, why would you need to ask for more? If it is not broken, don't fix it!

B B SALES CONNECTIONS

One on One Meeting Planner

Enter information in the yellow boxes to create your One on One Meeting Planner

Sales Representative	Sam Sales Representative
Date	Monday, July 20, 2009
Date of Next Meeting	Monday, July 27, 2009

Expected Sales To Close Before Next Meeting

Company	Plan of Action	Purpose of Call
ABC Company	Face to face meeting	Pick up signed contracts
123 Profit Inc	Phone call	Follow up on customer faxing contracts

---

But what if it is broken? What if the sales representative is working hard at what appears to be the right sales activities, but is still not producing the required sales results? The question is not whether something needs to be fixed, the question is what!

It has been said that the toughest part about solving a problem is actually uncovering the problem itself. You need to treat the problem, not just its symptoms. Nothing could be truer than when trying to improve the sales results of a struggling sales representative. You could spend a lot of time and effort in fixing what you think is the issue, but the sales representative might not actually improve his sales results.

For example, a common issue is that a sales representative is reporting they are doing the right number of prospecting calls but they are not getting the results to show for it. Before you bang your fist on your desk, demanding they do more calls, stop! You need to know why this is happening first. Is it that they are in the right place but not at the right time, or is it that they simply are not in the right place to begin with? Is it that they are not contacting the right people when they are prospecting, or is it that they are not contacting them in the right way? Quite simply, you need more information.

To help you pinpoint issues, you could use a more detailed sales report, one which gives you more information and facilitates a better discussion with your sales representative. You could also use more detailed reports for junior sales people who have just begun their careers in business to business sales as they will need a more structured environment in which to learn. It is better for them to develop the right works habits early in their sales career, as opposed to you trying to break their bad habits later.

The *Detailed Weekly Sales Report Worksheet* is an Excel workbook that contains five separate worksheets, examples of which are shown on the next few pages. When used together, these worksheets allow you to not only monitor your sales representatives' activities, but also see how they are doing them. Because you are now tracking the "how", you can see what is working and what is not. With this detail, you can quickly uncover problems, not just symptoms.

The first worksheet is called the *Weekly Sales Activity Tracking Worksheet*. It tracks the sales activities of a sales representative at each stage of the sales process, in relation to specified activity goals. In the example on the next page, the representative is completing the required prospecting calls, however is not booking enough appointments. Perhaps, he needs to spend more time prospecting new contacts as opposed to focusing on current customers, or vice versa, depending on your specific situation.

B B SALES CONNECTIONS

Weekly Sales Activity Tracking Worksheet

Enter information in the yellow boxes to track and monitor your weekly sales activities.

Sales Representative:	Sam Sales Representative
Week Ending:	Friday, July 24, 2009
Initial Monthly Sales Forecast:	$25,000

Sales to Date:	$38,650
Balance of Month Forecast:	$12,500
Revised Monthly Sales Forecast:	$51,150

Activity	Monday	Tuesday	Wednesday	Thursday	Friday	Total	(+/-)
Prospecting: Current Customers							
Goal	2	2	2	2	2	10	
Telemarketing Calls Completed	2	1	2	1	2	8	
Site Visits Completed	0	0	1	0	1	2	
Sub Total Calls Completed	2	1	3	1	3	10	0
Prospecting: New Contacts							
Goal	10	10	10	10	10	50	
Telemarketing Calls Completed	12	8	6	9	14	49	
Site Visits Completed	1	2	0	2	2	7	
Sub Total Calls Completed	13	10	6	11	16	56	6
Follow-up Callbacks from Prospect List							
Telemarketing Calls Completed	3	2	1	2	1	9	
Site Visits Completed	1	0	0	1	0	2	
Sub Total Calls Completed	4	2	1	3	1	11	N/A
Summary of All Prospecting Activities							
Total of Prospecting Calls	19	13	10	15	20	77	
Goal for Appointments Booked	2	2	2	2	2	10	
Actual Appointments Booked	3	1	2	1	0	7	(3)
Fact Finds Completed							
Goal	1	1	1	1	1	5	
Actual	1	0	1	0	1	3	(2)
Presentations of Offer Completed							
Goal	1	0	1	0	1	3	
Actual	0	1	0	0	1	2	(1)
Sales Closed							
Number of Sales Goal	0	1	0	1	0	2	
Number of Sales Actual	1	0	0	0	0	1	(1)
Sales Goal	$0	$6,250	$0	$6,250	$0	$12,500	
Sales Actual	$10,000	$0	$0	$0	$0	$10,000	($2,500)

The second worksheet is the *Sales Process Summary Worksheet*. It tracks actual prospects through the sales process, including what step has been completed, what is the next one, when it will take place. You need to make sure that the sales representative is not leaving one stage of the sales process without planning to move to the next.

This worksheet is most useful when compared to previous reports. By tracking specific prospects week after week, trends will emerge that will help you pinpoint problems. For example, if the representative booked appointments last week that were to have taken place this week, but those appointments did not happen, you are going to want to discuss why. Or if there are many fact finds being completed but no dates of presentations listed, then the sales representative may be forgetting to actually book these appointments before leaving the meetings. Or if the sales representative is presenting many offers, but is not closing sales nor listing the next steps to move the sales forward, perhaps they are not concluding their presentation meeting properly. Either way, by using this worksheet and the information it provides, you are much closer to improving the results of the sales representative.

B B SALES CONNECTIONS

Sales Process Summary Worksheet

Enter information in the yellow boxes to complete your Sales Process Summary Worksheet

Appointments Booked from Prospecting Activities

Company	Date Booked	Date of Appointment	Lead Source
ABC Company	20-Jul-2009	27-Jul-2009	Telemarketing New Contact
My Retirement Fund Group	24-Jul-2009	31-Jul-2009	Site Visit Current Customer

Fact Finds Completed

Company	Date Completed	Date of Presentation	Product of Interest	Size of Possible Sale
123 Profit Corp	21-Jul-2009	28-Jul-2009	Widget	$6,589

Presentations of Offer Completed

Company	Date Completed	Next Step To Complete Sale	Date of Next Step	Rating of Closing This Month
Encounter Enterprises	23-Jul-2009	Product Demo	15-Aug-2009	0%
Wants-to-Buy Today Inc	24-Jul-2009	Obtain Contracts	31-Jul-2009	95%

Sales Closed

Company	Date Completed	Product Sold	Size of Sale	Notes
SuperSales Inc	20-Jul-2009	Gadget	$10,000	Woo Hoo!

You will notice that the Presentation of Offers Completed section of the Sales Process Summary asks for a "Rating of Closing This Month" for each prospect. In this section, the sales representative should include a percentage indicating the chances that the sale will close this month. You are not asking whether the sale is forecast to close some time in the future, you are asking whether it will close *this month*. Again, you want your sales representative to focus only on the current time frame.

When using percentages to rate possible sales, it is important to define what each percentage means. Otherwise, every sales representative will have a different definition, making the ranking system useless. You will not be able to compare and combine the forecasts from each sales person to make one total sales forecast for your entire team.

A sample ranking system for sales forecasting is outlined below.

Rating of Closing This Month	Definition of Rating
0 %	There is no chance of the sale closing within the current month. You are not saying it will not be completed, you're saying it will not be completed *this month*.
25 %	It is unlikely that the sale will close this month because the sales process is not far enough along, or because the customer is unsure of his vendor of choice or the time frame of the sale.
50 %	It's a coin toss. The customer may or may not buy this month. Even if you have verbal confirmation that the sales will happen this month, the prospect may buy from you or they may buy from the competition.
75 %	You have received verbal confirmation that you are the vendor of choice, and you have received verbal confirmation that the sale will be completed this month; however the closing interview has yet to be scheduled.
95 %	The customer has given verbal approval that they will buy from you, and the closing interview appointment has been scheduled within the current month. The customer knows that the purpose of the appointment is to complete the order paperwork and finalize the sale.
100 %	Customer has signed all the required paperwork and the sale has been submitted to order processing.

The same ranking system should be used on the *Sales Funnel and Forecast Worksheet*, the third worksheet in your detailed sales report. It is a summary of the current month's sales funnel and forecast. It should be updated regularly with the previous sales activities. In other words, this is a summary of the sales representative's *Sales Process Summary Worksheets*.

B SALES CONNECTIONS

Sales Funnel and Forecast Worksheet

Enter information in the yellow boxes to track your Sales Funnel and create your Sales Forecast.

Sales Representative: Sam Sales Rep   Week Ending: Friday, July 24, 2009

Company	Appointment Booked?	Fact Find Completed?	Presentation of Offer Completed?	Sales Completed?	Product	Size of Sale	% of Closing This Month	Expected Closing Date of Date of Next Step
SuperSales Inc	Y	Y	Y	Y	Gadget	$10,000	100%	Closed
Wants-to-Buy Today Inc.	Y	Y	Y		Widget	$7,500	95%	31-Jul-2009
Encounter Enterprises	Y	Y	Y		Whachamacallit	$4,560	0%	15-Aug-2009
123 Profit Corp	Y	Y			Widget	$6,589	0%	10-Sep-2009
My Retirement Fund Group	Y				Gadget	$2,500	0%	31-Jul-2009
ABC Company	Y				Whachamacallit	$8,895	0%	27-Jul-2009

The fourth worksheet in the detailed sales report is the *One on One Meeting Planner*. Similar to the form discussed earlier, this worksheet creates a plan of action to move prospects forward in the sales process.

Expected Sales To Close This Week

Company	Plan of Action	Purpose of Call

Follow-up On Hot Prospects This Week

Company	Plan of Action	Purpose of Call

Action Items to Be Completed This Week

Action Item	Plan of Action	To Be Completed By

Other Objectives, Comments, and To-Do's

The difference with this version is that it has been modified to be used in a weekly one on one meeting as opposed to a monthly. The key is to have your sales representative focus only on the upcoming week and let their follow up file systems manage the rest.

The fifth and final worksheet in the detailed sales report is the *Next Week's Weekly Appointment Calendar*. This is a tool to help you manage how your sales representative is planning their time. As stated earlier, we can't change the past. We want to assess not only what happened last week, but also be able to coach them on what is planned for the upcoming week.

You want your sales representatives to arrive at the office Monday morning with their week already booked. To do this, they must work this week to book next week's activities. If you want to see who on your team is planning ahead this way, call a mandatory sales meeting for 10:00 am tomorrow. Was it your top performers who complained the most about the short notice? Those who did not complain are the ones who need help on their time management. If they can attend your meeting on such short notice, that means they didn't have any appointments with customers.

Sales representatives should use a calendar which shows a whole week on one page. The only way to plan a week properly is to be able to see the entire week at a glance. If your sales people are using a PDA that cannot show this, you must require them to use the *Next Week's Appointment Calendar* worksheet below. If they are using a different type of calendar that shows the week at a glance, then they can simply photocopy it and submit that to you instead.

Notice that the worksheet concentrates on the upcoming week, not the week past. Again, you want them to focus on what is to be done, not what has already happened and cannot be changed.

The first thing entered into the calendar are booked appointments, including meetings with customers, sales meetings and personal appointments. When doing so, the sales representative should also write in the geographic location of each appointment using the postal code.

Next, the sales representative should book time for office duties. This should be in non-peak selling hours like first thing in the morning of after 4 pm in the afternoon. Preparing quotes, answering emails, and completing sales paperwork should be completed in this scheduled time, but only in this scheduled time and not in prime selling hours.

Most importantly, time should be booked in for prospecting activities. It should be stressed to the sales representative that this is a scheduled appointment just like a meeting with a prospect. They would not consider canceling a customer call; therefore they should not cancel on themselves and their future sales success by failing to complete their prospecting activities.

When your sales representative prospects this week, they should look to fill the holes in next week's calendar. New appointments should be booked in the same geographical locations as the existing ones to minimize unproductive travel time. Proper planning this way will allow your sales representatives to fit more into their sales day.

B B SALES CONNECTIONS

Next Week's Appointment Calendar

Enter information in the yellow boxes to your weekly appointments.

Sales Representative: Sam Sales Rep

Week Ending: Friday, July 31, 2009

Time	Monday	Tuesday	Wednesday	Thursday	Friday
Date	27-Jul-09	28-Jul-09	29-Jul-09	30-Jul-09	31-Jul-09
7:00 AM					
7:30 AM					
8:00 AM					
8:30 AM	Sales Meeting	Office Work	Office Work	Office Work	Office Work
9:00 AM		Telemarketing & Follow Up Sales Calls	Telemarketing & Follow Up Sales Calls	Telemarketing & Follow Up Sales Calls	Telemarketing & Follow Up Sales Calls
9:30 AM	Telemarketing & Follow Up Sales Calls				
10:00 AM					
10:30 AM		123 Profit Corp Presentation of Offer -			My Retirement Group Fund Fact Find - K4V
11:00 AM	ABC Company Fact Find				
11:30 AM					Prospecting & Customer Site Visit Calls in Postal Code K4V
12:00 PM			Prospecting & Customer Site Visit Calls in Postal Code K1P	Prospecting & Customer Site Visit Calls in Postal Code K1P	
12:30 PM					
1:00 PM	Prospecting & Customer Site Visit Calls in Postal Code K2J	Prospecting & Customer Site Visit Calls in Postal Code K2G			Wants-To-Buy Inc - Pick Up Signed Contracts K4Z
1:30 PM					
2:00 PM					Prospecting & Customer Site Visit Calls in Postal Code K4Z
2:30 PM					
3:00 PM					
3:30 PM	Follow Up Telephone	Follow Up Telephone	Follow Up Telephone	Follow Up Telephone	Follow Up Telephone
4:00 PM	Office Work	Office Work	Office Work	Office Work	Office Work
4:30 PM					
5:00 PM					
5:30 PM					
6:00 PM					
6:30 PM					
7:00 PM					

To Do List	To Do List	To Do List	To Do List	To Do List
Send 10 Prospecting	Send 10 Prospecting	Send 10 Prospecting	Send 10 Prospecting	Send 10 Prospecting
Prepare Quote for ABC Company				Submit Order from Wants-To-Buy

Some sales representatives see more detailed sales reports as nothing more than a policing action. "The boss is just checking up on me to ensure that I am doing my prospecting calls." Let's face it, as sales manager, you already know if they are making their calls or not. Their sales results, or lack thereof, are already telling you that. The most successful sales representatives look at sales reports differently. They see them as tools to monitor if they are on track to reach their goals. They also know that activity tracking can uncover areas for improvement so they can be even more successful in the future.

If you think of detailed sales reports at a GPS navigation system to help your representatives get where they want to go, their buy in to the reporting system will be much higher. Therefore you actually have to communicate to your sales representatives that they are heading in the right direction. Write comments on the report and return it to representative in addition to discussing them in your one on one meetings. They have to know that you are actually reviewing them and they are not just submitting them as an exercise in futility.

Performance Reviews

In order to be successful in the long term, a sales manager must manage their team to create a win-win between the employer and employee. The organization must be achieving its goals, and so must the sales professional. A Performance Reviews is where this win-win relationship is discussed in detail.

A Performance Review is essentially a more formalized one on one meeting with your sales representative. It normally covers a longer time frame and discusses broader goals and objectives.   For example, a one on one meeting covers daily activity objectives on a weekly or monthly basis, whereas a performance review would cover overall quota attainment on a yearly basis.

It is recommended to hold Performance Reviews at the following times:

- At the end of a new hire's probationary period
- At the start of a new sales year with each sales representative
- When there is a performance issue with a sales representative and the previously discussed management tools have not improved results

The agenda for the Performance Review is contained in the *Performance Review Worksheet*. This Excel workbook contains different worksheets, some of which should be prepared by the sales representative before the meeting, with others to be prepared by you. The end result of all the worksheets will be an accurate assessment of the sales representative's performance, coupled with a plan of action for the future.

- Personal Goal Definition Worksheet – This is the same worksheet discussed earlier in the training course. As time moves forward, goals and aspirations change and therefore this worksheet should be reviewed and adjusted regularly. The sales representative should update this ahead of time and should be prepared to discuss the Career and Educational Goals section at the meeting.

Step 3 - Career & Educational Goals	
Next 12 Months	Become B2B Sales Connection Accredited, Make quota, Earn the trip to Presidents Club
Next 2 - 4 Years	Earn a promotion to sales management, Take an adult education course in public speaking
Long Term	Earn a promotion to senior management

- Goal Setting & Action Planning Worksheet – This worksheet, also discussed earlier, should be updated by the sales representative prior to the meeting as well. As their sales skills improve, the daily activity required to make a sale would change. This will be very important information to have in order to make plans for the future.

What is the total annual income you wish to earn to fund your lifestyle?	$ 100,000.00
What is your base salary?	$ 50,000.00
What is your average monthly bonus earned?	$ 500.00
What is your average commission rate?	8%
What is your average size sale?	$ 10,000.00
How many presentations does it take you to make a sale?	3.0
How many fact finds does it take you to make a presentation?	2.0
How many prospecting calls does it take you to book a fact find?	15.0
Total Annual Sales Volume Required for Goal Attainment	$ 550,000.00
Total Monthly Sales Volume Required for Goal Attainment	$ 45,833.33
Number of Sales Required Per Month	5
Number of Sales Required Per Week	1.25
Number of Presentations Required Per Month	15
Number of Presentations Required Per Week	3.75
Number of Fact Finds Required Per Month	30
Number of Fact Finds Required Per Week	7.50
Number of Prospecting Calls Required Per Month	450
Number of Prospecting Calls Required Per Week	113
Number of Prospecting Calls Required Per Day	23

- Sales Performance & Action Plan Worksheet – The first section of this worksheet should be prepared by you prior to the meeting. This is an assessment of the sales representative's performance in relation to the assigned targets. The second section is to be completed at the meeting together with your sales representative. It combines the sales representative's personal objectives with their assigned targets, and gives you a discussion forum to agree to a plan of action to attain them.

Sales Performance Review & Action Planning Worksheet

B&B SALES CONNECTIONS

Enter information in yellow boxes to complete the worksheet.

Sales Representative:	Sam Sales Representative
Sales Manager:	Mathew Manager
Date:	Monday, January 04, 2010

Section 1 - Previous Time Period's Sales Performance Review

Objective	Goal	Actual	Percentage Attainment
Yearly Sales Quota	$ 1,000,000.00	$ 1,010,000.00	101.0%
New Customers Obtained	24	26	108.3%
Earn President's Club Status	$ 1,100,000.00	$ 1,010,000.00	91.8%

Section 2 - Action Planning

Objective	Recommended Action	Support & Resources Needed	Measurements of Success	Time Frame
Earn President's Club	Increase daily activity	20 Calls Per Day	Weekly Reports	All Year
	Improve order processing accurancy	Training on proper paperwork	Decrease in order processing time	1/31/2010
	Increase average size sale	Training on add on sales	10 % increase in average sale size	12/31/2010
Prmotion into sales management	Take Sales Management Course	Management course to be purchased	B2B Sales Connections Accreditation	6/30/2010
	Mentor junior sales rep	Manager to assign junior rep	20 % increase in junior reps sales performance	
	Improve public speaking skills	Join Toastmasters Club	6 Toastmaster Speeaches	12/31/2010

The complete *Performance Review Worksheet* workbook should be signed by both you and the representative as an indication of your commitments to making it happen. The representative should be given a copy, and you should keep a copy in the representative's personnel file for future reference. By doing so, you are both agreeing that you are on the same page and will be moving in the same direction to achieve your common goals.

Sales Incentive Contests

Sales contests are extremely common tools used by sales managers. In fact, you would be hard pressed to walk into any sales office and discover a sales manager who is not running some sort of contest to motivate his team to increase productivity. You probably wouldn't find any of the two contests exactly the same either.

Why not run a sales contest? They're always fun, rewarding, a good change of pace from the every day routine, and they always make money, right? Wrong! Before you jump in with your check book wide open, the fact is not all sales contests motivate, and not all are profitable. In fact, if not designed properly, contests can do more harm than good.

The biggest mistake you can make as a sales manager is to design a contest that only has a single winner. Having experienced these contests both as a direct sales representative and as part of a management team, a "winner takes it all" qualification should be avoided at all costs, and that is speaking from the winner's point of view!

The reason is that these contests tend to be won by the same sales representative time after time. The feeling on the team then becomes "why should I put the extra effort in, Sam always wins anyway." Even if the contest is more competitive with different representatives having a chance to win, if someone gets out to an early lead, others will stop competing if they think the lead is insurmountable. Either way, the contest that was supposed to create fun and increase motivation has actually done the complete opposite.

Some managers have tried to alleviate this problem by having contests where the top three or top five sales representatives all win. In reality, where ever you draw the line, the same issues exist. In this case, you may have created motivation among your top representatives to compete with one another, but what about the rest of your team? The best contests are those designed to motivate all of your representatives to compete within themselves while creating a financial benefit for the company.

Again, speaking from experience, by a wide margin, the most motivating and most productive sales contests are those where everyone on the team can qualify and win as opposed to having just one winner. In other words, you set a target, and whoever reaches it, wins. Not only does this keep everyone engaged in the contest longer, it actually produces more sales overall!

You may be thinking because you have both senior and junior sales people, a qualification target system like this will not work in your situation. It's true that your top producers should have to stretch to reach higher targets than those who are new to the team however, the system can still work. All you need is a handicapping system so that qualification is fair for everyone. In fact, you probably already have such a system. It's called a sales quota.

If your sales quotas are already adjusted based on territory opportunity, experience or previous sales results, then all you have to do is make qualification a percentage of quota. For example, everyone who reaches 110 percent of their quota wins. If your quotas are the same for everyone, then perhaps your sales contest doesn't need to be handicapped in the first place. If you believe it does, be creative. Where there's a will, there's a way.

The second biggest mistake made by sales managers when creating sales contests is not setting the bar high enough. They actually lose money when a prize is awarded. The goal is to make the qualification targets high enough that the sales representatives have to stretch to reach them, yet low enough that they are both attainable and profitable.

It is worth noting at this point, there is no prize too outrageous or too expensive to offer the winners. Whatever the cost, you just need to plan properly to ensure that you receive the right amount of sales required to earn it. You must factor in the appropriate profit to make the prize cost effective. The *Sales Contest Target Quota Calculation Worksheet* is an Excel workbook that will help you do that.

In the example shown on the next page, the sales contest prize costs $100,000 per representative. The cost, however, is completely irrelevant as long as the increase in sales produced justifies the expense. If the sales target is set high enough to pay the cost of the prize, as well as the cost of the goods sold and the resulting commissions, the contest will be profitable. In this case, as long as the incremental sales generated is higher than the breakeven sales level of $312,500, the contest will have been worth while.

You may be thinking that expensive sales contest prizes are ludicrous, but they do produce results. For example, there's the true story about one business owner, who after calculating the costs and adding a healthy profit for the company, launched a sales contest where he offered a Porsche™ to anyone on his team who hit their assigned targets. Did it work? Five out of the six sales representatives on the team drove away from the sales meeting the following year in their new sports cars!

Sales Contest Target Quota Calculation Worksheet

B B SALES CONNECTIONS

Enter data in the yellow boxes to calculate the sales contest target quota per sales representative.

Annual Sales Quota Per Representative.	$ 1,000,000
Contest Length in Months	12
Commission Rate As A Percentage of Gross Margin Per Representative	20.0%
Desired Incremental Gross Profit From Contest Per Representative	$ 50,000
Total Cost of Contest Prize Per Representative	$ 100,000
Product Selling Price	$ 10,000
Less Cost of Goods Sold	$ 6,000
Gross Profit	$ 4,000
Less Sales Compensation	$ 800
Less Other Variable Costs	$ -
Contribution to Fixed Costs	$ 3,200
Gross Profit Margin	40.0%
Contribution To Fixed Costs Margin	32.0%
Incremtal Sales Required Per Representative For Contest To Break Even	$ 312,500
Incremental Sales Required Per Representative To Reach Profit Target	$ 468,750
Regular Sales Quota For Same Time Frame	$ 1,000,000.00
Total Sales Quota Per Representative for Sales Contest	$ 1,468,750

The sales contest target worksheet assumes that you know your commission rate as a percentage of your gross margin. If you only know your commission rate as a percentage of sales, the conversion worksheet also contained in the *Sales Contest Target Quota Calculation Worksheet* workbook will calculate this for you.

Gross Profit Compensation Conversion Worksheet

B B SALES CONNECTIONS

Enter data in the yellow boxes to convert the overall amount of sales compensation to a percentage of gross profit

Commission Rate As A Persentatge of Sales	8.0%
Product Selling Price	$ 1,000.00
Less Cost of Goods Sold	$ 600.00
Gross Profit	$ 400.00
Sales Compensation As A Percentage of Gross Profit	20.0%

Another true story speaks to a sales manager who, after making his calculations, offered all expenses paid family vacations. In this contest, not only did every member of the sales team end up soaking up the Caribbean sun in the middle of a Canadian winter, but the company also made more profits overall than if they had only offered one prize to one winner.

When choosing prizes, think about what's motivating to your team. In our examples, fancy sports cars worked for young singles in a big city, and vacations worked for families with small children. Remember, it's not a matter of the prize that you want to give; it's a matter of the prize your team wants to earn. Sometimes a big effort just requires a bigger carrot.

Just as the prize is important, so is the way in which you communicate a representative's progress towards winning it. Throughout your contest, publish results and the progress of everyone on the team. Put up posters and send out email updates regularly. One sales manager mailed sun glasses with a hand written note to the representatives' spouses when they were getting close to qualifying for a family vacation. Be creative. The more excitement you can generate, the better. In fact, many managers believe that the communication about the contest is more important than the prize itself.

When publishing the results, don't just report how much has been sold so far, but also how much more needs to be sold to qualify. If a contest runs across a number of months, break down the larger target into smaller ones that cover shorter time frames. For example, if a sales representative needs to sell $21,000 in 3 months, let him know that he needs $7,000 per month to qualify. When a representative does qualify, make a very public announcement about it. It is very motivating to others on the team when they hear of someone who has won.

Sales contests have been and will continue to be effective ongoing management tools. They can be based on actual sales as discussed, or they can be based on sales activities that are required to generate sales. You can set targets for a certain number of prospecting calls or fact finding appointments within a given time frame, or you can set a specified number of new customers a sales person needs to acquire as a qualification.

Whatever prize or qualification requirement you decide on for your sales contest, if you make it motivating, and if you make it profitable, and then you communicate the results, you will have made it successful.

Other Sales Management Tools

We have all heard the old saying that necessity is the mother of invention. This certainly is true in many sales organizations. Some of the best ongoing management tools were created because a sales manager had a problem to solve.

Below are a number of other tools which have been used successfully by sales managers over the years to teach, coach or motivate their teams to become better sales professionals.

Blitz Days

Blitz Days are very common in some industries, yet never attempted in others. A blitz day is essentially when everyone on the sales team sets aside time to prospect all at the same time, either on the telephone or face to face prospecting. If you are looking ahead and seeing that the sales funnel has not had anything new poured into it for a while, a blitz day is a great solution. If your company has never launched a blitz, maybe it's time you did.

A few of the best opportunities to run a blitz day are listed below.

- When the team needs to generate many new prospects in a very short period of time.
- If you launch a new product and you want to get the word out to the marketplace very quickly.
- Following up on a marketing initiative like a direct mail campaign

On the day of the blitz, have everyone meet at the office in the morning for a quick kick off meeting, and then starts prospecting together. You could announce that there will be some small prizes like restaurant gift certificates to those who hit specified activity targets during the blitz. Or every appointment booked could earn a lottery ticket for a chance to win a grand prize. You could end the day with a team dinner where the winners are presented with their prizes and the sales results are announced.

Blitzing in teams is very common. You can pair up a junior and senior sales representative together so that the whole experience becomes a training opportunity in addition to a lead generating exercise. The teams could spend half the day in one representative's territory, and then switch to their partner's territory in the afternoon.

Some managers conduct full blitz days every month or quarter, while others prefer half day blitzes every week. Whatever the time frame you choose, if you need a quick influx of new prospects, you can never go wrong with a blitz day.

Automated Sales Tools

Many studies show that sales representatives only spend about 25 percent of their time selling. The rest of their time is spent on order processing, administration, customer service and travel. To put that into perspective, your team is actually only selling ten hours a week or 500 hours a year.

Taking this fact a step further, if your representatives have a $1 million quota, then each of your sales people are expected to produce $2,000 in revenue for each hour of selling time. Now imagine how much more your team would produce if you could free up just one more hour a week for each of your representatives to spend on selling.

One of the best ways to increase selling productivity is with automation. Any routine task that is done over and over by your sales representatives can and should be automated, saving time and reducing the opportunity for errors. Automatic price calculators, order entry sheets, and quote templates are just a few excellent examples of tools that reduce the time spent on administration, therefore freeing up more time to spend on selling.

For example, if you always have to add shipping costs to an order, don't have the sales person calculate it, just build it into the price in the first place. If you need to have the cost breakdown for accounting purposes, remember it is cheaper to hire administrative help or to create a spreadsheet to break it out automatically than it is to spend selling time calculating it.

Have you ever thought to yourself "it certainly would save time if only my team had a tool to do this"? Then create it. If it will require you to make a financial investment, remember that every hour freed for selling earns you $2,000. At that rate of return, chances are the investment is a good one.

Remember, the only difference between a good idea and a great idea is implementation. What's the definition of implementation? It's the sales manager who follows it through to the end!

Discounting Policies

Experience has shown no matter where you set your minimum selling price, a sales representative sooner or later will ask you to lower it. The question is not whether you will be asked permission to discount; the question is when do you say yes.

Your company's fixed costs must be paid whether you make the sale or not. Therefore, any time a discounted selling price contributes at least one dollar towards paying your fixed costs, it is considered worthwhile. As long as all of your variable costs are covered, including the cost of the goods sold plus any variable sales commissions, the discounted price can be accepted.

The *Minimum Selling Price Calculation Worksheet* will automatically calculate a product's minimum selling price to contribute at least one dollar towards the payment of fixed costs, given the cost of goods sold and the commissions to be paid on the sale. As most managers would agree that making a sale for only a dollar is hardly worth the effort, the spreadsheet also shows how much gross profit is being made if you sell the product at a certain price.

B B SALES CONNECTIONS

Minimum Selling Price Calculation Worksheet

Enter data in the yellow boxes to calculate a product's minimum selling price.	
Requested Discounted Selling Price	$ 8,000
Cost of Goods Sold	$ 6,000
Commissions To Be Paid on Sale At Requested Price	$ 1,500
Gross Profit Contibution to Fixed Costs	$ 500
Minimum Product Selling Price	$ 7,501

As you can see, even if a discounted price is more than the cost of goods sold, you must always consider other variable selling costs like sales commissions when calculating your final selling price.

If you and your sales representative both feel that you have to give something more to a customer to "close the deal", give away something that is considered a fixed cost as an alternative to a price discount. For example, if you have a product trainer who is paid a fixed salary, give the customer an extra product training session at no charge. Not only does this bring great value to the customer, but it actually costs you nothing since you have to pay the trainer whether they conduct the extra training session or not.

If a sales representative insists that the product must be sold below the calculated minimum selling price, you only have two choices. One is you can say no, or two is to adjust the commissions payable downward. To do otherwise would be to lose money and that is just not good business sense. The bottom line is the bottom line!

A sales manager on a new assignment soon discovered that his sales team was too quick to give price discounts. The company had never questioned the practice in the past, so it simply had become the norm. After careful research, the manager instituted a new policy where the sales person could authorize a discount, but the result would be a decrease in the commission rate paid on the sale.

The new policy caused a great cry of outrage in the sales department, with predictions of doom for the company. Within 30 days of instituting the new policy, the discounts stopped because of its direct impact on the sales representatives' pay. The company's profit increased. Sales did not suffer, in fact the average sales value increased. Sometimes you just need to change the behavior.

Ongoing Training Meetings

Informal ongoing training meetings are a great way to keep your sales representatives learning and developing their skills. The key is to keep them short, unstructured, and run them either first thing in the morning or at the end of the day so they do not interfere with peak selling hours.

The meetings could focus on a variety of topics, ranging from product knowledge, to operations, to sales skills. They could also be an idea sharing session resulting from the events of the previous sales day.

One sales manager had a half hour product training meeting every day at 8:00 am. This way, the meetings were over before the sales day began. There was no formal agenda. In fact, the representative's questions often determined the topics discussed on any given day. Basically, the sales manager was just making himself available to help anyone who wanted to improve their product knowledge. Attendance was not mandatory, just those who wanted to learn showed up. Interestingly enough, as the sales results of the sales representatives who attended these meetings improved, attendance grew.

Outside Training Courses

If you do not have the proper skill set, or if your resources are simply stretched too thin to properly train a sales representative, then it is best to outsource the task. Training courses provided by outside third parties, either paid upfront by the company or reimbursed to the employee after completion, are a great way to develop the skills and knowledge of your sales people across a variety of areas.

Perhaps your representative would better understand the needs of your high tech customers if they took a computer course. Or perhaps an advanced selling course would be of benefit to you booth. If the sales representative has aspirations to move upward in your organization, a sales management or general business course might be appropriate. Some companies have even been known to pay for MBA degrees for their aspiring executives.

As a sales manager, your sales people are your customers. The best way to service your customers is to help them get to where they want to go, whether that involves improving their sales results or making them upwardly mobile within your organization. An investment that helps them get to where they want to go will also reap you rewards in the long run by giving you better educated, more productive sales professionals.

Association Memberships

There is a professional association for virtually every industry imaginable. Chambers of Commerce, Boards of Trade, industry trade and professional sales associations are just a few examples. Joining these associations is usually inexpensive, especially when you consider the increased visibility you and your sales team will realize in the local business community.

In addition to these associations being a great way to network and generate business, they also provide a great knowledge base for your sales team. Most associations have regularly scheduled events like breakfast networking meetings where they schedule expert guest speakers to discuss a wide variety of topics. Get on the mailing list of the association and check their website often. When an interesting topic comes up, you can treat your whole sales team.

If you are not physically close to a local chapter, most have excellent online communities and social networks on websites like LinkedIn™ as well. Check your local yellow pages under "Associations" or perform a quick internet search and you will be certain to find an association that is relevant and interests you and your sales team.

WHEN TO UNHIRE

Sometimes, even when the sales manager does everything right, the organization and the sales professional must part ways. This could be the employee's choice, or this could be the employer's choice.

Please remember, all companies and managers should seek legal advice as it applies to their federal, provincial or state employment and labour laws before making decisions or taking actions in this area. This section is designed to assist you in dealing with Human Resources issues but is not to be considered legal advice.

Resignations are a fact of life in this business. If this has not happened to you yet, it will eventually. If a member on your team resigns, it is because they feel that they can better accomplish their personal goals elsewhere. You can do everything in your power to help a sales person get to where they want to go, but sometimes they just believe that the grass is greener on the other side of the fence. If you can't change that perception, wish the sales person success in their future and move on.

The real question is, as sales manager, when should you make the decision to sever the employer employee relationship? To answer this, you first must ask yourself if the nonperforming sales representative knows what needs to be done to be successful. Do they know how many calls need to completed, how many fact finds, etc?

If the answer is yes, they know what to do, then the second question you need to ask is if they know how. Does the sales representative know how to make a prospecting call? Do they know what questions to ask in a fact find, etc? If they don't, then using the techniques discussed in this training course, show them. Often, the problem with lack of performance, when it comes right down to it, is they don't know how, and your job is to teach them. If you point a finger at a sales representative to tell them they are doing a bad job, there are always three fingers pointing back at you.

However, if the sales representative knows what to do to sell, and you believe they know how to do sell because you have seen them do it first hand, you must ask yourself one last question. Do they want to? Are they prepared to do what it takes to be a successful sales professional in your organization? If you get to this last question and the answer is no, there is not much more you can do.

No one likes to fire anyone. In fact, once you have done it once, it will teach you to hire better in the first place so you don't have to do it often. The fact remains however, it is sometimes in everyone's best interests to go your separate ways. The sales representative is not happy as they are not reaching their personal goals, and neither are you.

It will cost you more in the long run to have the wrong sales representation in a sales territory than it will to not have any representation there at all. Don't make the mistake of believing that hanging onto a nonperforming sales person is a better choice than taking the time and effort to hire a new, more productive one. If you have done everything you can, it will not get better!

SAMPLE TERMINATION OF EMPLOYMENT WITHIN PROBATIONARY PERIOD LETTER

August 7, 2009

Samual A. Representative
123 Any Street
Toronto, ON
H0H 0H0

> **Disclaimer**: Always check with legal counsel before using this template to insure you comply with your local labour & employment requirements.

Dear Sam:

This letter will serve to confirm our meeting today during which we advised you of the termination of your employment with _____. This is in accordance with the three-month introductory period clause as outlined in your offer of employment dated _____.

Your employment is terminated effective immediately and you will be paid up to and including today. We will compensate you for any vacation pay or qualifying business expenses that may remain owing to you as of your last day. Any employment separation paperwork that is required will be mailed to you.

You must immediately return all property to which you agreed were to be returned to the company upon request or termination of employment. This includes but is not limited to access cards, keys and computer related equipment. For the assets that you do not have with you now, we trust that you will ensure their safe return to us as soon as possible.

We wish you the very best in your career transition efforts.

Sincerely,

Once you have reached the decision to sever the employment relationship, it is easiest if it is within the employee's probationary period as outlined in your initial offer of employment letter. As shown in this sample termination letter, and depending on your local employment laws, you may simply be able to inform the employee in writing that their employment will not be continued after the probationary period. There is no need to explain if you do not wish to, you just need to ensure that you give the appropriate notification before the probationary period expires.

If you wish to terminate an employee who is past their initial probationary period, the process usually takes place over a longer time frame. In fact, anyone with a human resources background will tell you that you cannot just fire someone on the spur of the moment without "just cause". While laws do exists, you actually can fire anyone any time. It is just a matter of how much it is going to cost you. As most sales managers want to avoid huge severance settlements and wrongful dismissal lawsuits, we highly recommend you first seek legal advice and then follow a 60 day termination strategy.

The first step is to hold a Performance Review with the sales representative. At the conclusion, you must provide a 60 day warning letter to the sales representative similar to the letter on the next page. Please note that the contents of this letter must be based on the sales reports that the sales representative would have been submitting to you regularly. The better you have the performance and activities of the non performing sales representative documented in their personnel file, along with the steps you have taken to help them succeed, the easier and more legally sound the termination process will be.

If you have been holding regular one on one meetings with your representative, the poor sales results discussed at the Performance Review will not be a surprise to the representative. He may not like it, but he will not be surprised. If he refuses to sign the letter at the bottom acknowledging its receipt, note the refusal in your files.

The purpose of the warning letter is to provide a wake up call to the non performing sales representative so that sales results will improve. The sales person will either get to work and improve their sales, or they will immediately start looking at the classified ads and in the end, possible resigning before you terminate their employment. Either way, you both will be moving forward.

If sales results continue to be below company standards, you then hold another Performance Review again on the scheduled date where you present the sales representative a 30 day warning letter. If there still is no improvement, you can often terminate their employment one month later by providing a termination letter.

The amount of termination pay owed to the employee will depend on your local employment laws. Since the lack of sales performance would be well documented on the previous sales reports, as well as the two warning letters, you should not have to pay any more than the minimum required by law. If the representative threatens to sue for wrongful dismissal, your will have plenty of backup to prove that the employee was not performing at a level equal to your company's standards, and this was the cause for termination of employment.

Please note that in any termination process, you must have the employee return all company property to you. This could include office keys, customer lists, or laptop computers. Anything that was deemed to remain the company's property must be returned. Some employers have been known to hold onto the employees final paycheck until all the company property has been returned.

On the reverse, you will also have obligations to the former employee. You must provide them with all of the legally required separation papers and severance pay, and you must provide them the opportunity to gather their personal belongings before you escort them out of the building.

If you have any questions as to the exact wording of your warning letters, or your final termination letter, see the advice of an expert. As provincial and state laws vary, if you are unsure of what your legal rights and obligations are, it is always a worth while investment to consult your human resources department or outside legal council who specialize in employment law.

Regardless of how the employer employee relationship ended, be it by termination or resignation, it can happen very quickly. Even if the sales representative has given you two week's notice, it is customary to not accept it. The chances are that they will not be productive in that notification time anyway as they have already moved on mentally. Also, it is certainly not a good idea to have someone continue to represent your company to your customers if they have resigned to go to and work for your competition, or when they know they are being terminated in a few weeks.

As discussed in the recruiting section of this training course, you should always have access to a steady source of sales candidates. By having a virtual bench so to speak, you will always be prepared to start the recruiting process on a moments notice. The need to fill an empty territory is inevitable, and you should always be prepared for the inevitable.

SAMPLE 60 DAY WARNING LETTER

August 7, 2009

Samual A. Representative
123 Any Street
Toronto, ON
H0H 0H0

> **Disclaimer**: Always check with legal counsel before using this template to insure you comply with your local labour & employment requirements.

Dear Sam:

As discussed in our meeting today, your sales performance over the past three months is below the required standards and must be corrected immediately.

Specifically, your sales performance is as follows:
- May Sales Results - $43,500 versus quota of $83,333 or 52% attainment
- June Sales Results - $36,750 versus quota of $83,333 or 44% attainment
- July Sales Results – $59,360 versus quota of $83,333 or 71% attainment

Currently, your sales results year to date are only 63% of your assigned quota.

The following are my observations as to why your sales performance is below the required standards:
- Your weekly sales reports indicate that you are averaging only 5 prospecting calls per day, however most sales representatives need an average of at least 10 calls per day to succeed.
- You do not have sufficient sales that are forecasted at 75% or higher to close in any given month to reach quota. Most sales representatives need three times quota or $250,000 forecasted to succeed

As a result of your sales performance falling below 80% year to date, the following Action Plan is being initiated to bring your sales performance up to company standards. This program will remain in place for 30 day increments and will be reviewed with you monthly. These monthly reviews will indicate whether program continuance is warranted. My expectation of your performance and your goal should be achievement of 100% or higher of your assigned quota. This expected performance standard is no more or no less than is expected of any other sales representative.

The components of the Action Plan we are initiating for you are as follows:

You will report to me, weekly on Monday mornings at 8:00 am for a review of your activities of the week. This analysis will consist of:

- Reviewing your week's objectives and accomplishments in terms of sales activities
- Reviewing the new prospects found in your territory
- Reviewing your existing prospects in terms of progression through the sales process.
- Reviewing the growth in the prospects on your sales forecast ranked at 75% or higher of closing within the current month.

Minimum sales activity targets that must be met by you are as follows:

- Complete a minimum of 10 prospecting calls per day.
- Conduct of minimum of 1 fact find appointment per day
- Attend all team meetings and training sessions

Sam, your desire to succeed is critical to you achieving your goals. I am available to assist your efforts. If you have any questions, do not hesitate to ask. We will meet again 30 days on September 7, 2009 to discuss your progress.

Failure to meet the targets mentioned above and to successfully improve and sustain your performance could result in further corrective action, up to and including termination of employment.

Please sign below to acknowledge that the contents of this letter have been reviewed with you.

Sincerely,

Matthew Manager
Regional Sales Manager

_____   _____
Employee Signature   Date

CC: Human Resources Department

SAMPLE 30 DAY WARNING LETTER

August 7, 2009

Samual A. Representative
123 Any Street
Toronto, ON
H0H 0H0

> **Disclaimer**: Always check with legal counsel before using this template to insure you comply with your local labour & employment requirements.

Dear Sam:

As discussed in our meeting of August 7, 2009 and again today, your sales performance continues to be below the required standards and must be corrected immediately.

Specifically, your sales performance is as follows:
- June Sales Results - $36,750 versus quota of $83,333 or 44% attainment
- July Sales Results – $59,360 versus quota of $83,333 or 71% attainment
- August Sales Results - $47,620 versus quota of $83,333 or 57% attainment

Currently, your sales results year to date are only 56% of your assigned quota.

The following are my observations as to why your sales performance is below the required standards:
- Your weekly sales reports indicate that you are averaging only 7 prospecting calls per day versus the required minimum of 10.
- You are averaging only 3 fact finds per week versus the required minimum of 1 per day.

As your sales performance has not improved, the Action Plan initiated to bring your sales performance up to company standards on August 7 2009 will continue. My expectation of your performance and your goal should be achievement of 100% or higher of your assigned quota.

I am available to assist your efforts. If you have any questions, do not hesitate to ask. We will meet again 30 days on October 7, 2009 to discuss your progress.

Failure to meet the targets mentioned above and to successfully improve and sustain your performance could result in further corrective action, up to and including termination of employment.

Please sign below to acknowledge that the contents of this letter have been reviewed with you.

Sincerely,

Matthew Manager
Regional Sales Manager

_____   _____
Employee Signature   Date

CC: Human Resources Department

SAMPLE TERMINATION OF EMPLOYMENT AFTER PROBATIONARY PERIOD LETTER

August 7, 2009

Disclaimer: Always check with legal counsel before using this template to insure you comply with your local labour & employment requirements.

Samual A. Representative
123 Any Street
Toronto, ON H0H 0H0

Dear Sam:

This letter will serve to confirm our meeting today during which we advised you of the termination of your employment with _____. As discussed and confirmed to you in writing on _____ and _____, your sales performance is below company standards, and is the cause for your termination.

Your employment is terminated effective immediately, and you will be paid up to and including _____. This is the equivalent to _____ weeks pay in lieu of termination notice, and is in accordance with our legal requirements.

We will compensate you for any unused vacation pay as legally required, as well as any qualifying business expenses that may remain owing to you as of your last day. Your group benefits will continue for a period of _____ days. Any employment separation paperwork that is required will be mailed to you.

You must immediately return all property to which you agreed were to be returned to the company upon request or termination of employment. This includes but is not limited to access cards, keys and computer related equipment. For the assets that you do not have with you now, we trust that you will ensure their safe return to us as soon as possible.

We wish you the very best in your career transition efforts.

Sincerely,

Matthew Manager
Regional Sales Manager

CONCLUSION

As the sales manager, your job can best be described as that of a coach. You plan, you instruct, you lead and you motivate. You have many tools at your disposal to help you manage your operation. When used properly, these tools can be combined to build a very strong and successful team.

You don't actually play the game, you teach others to. In doing so, you develop each member of your team so that they may reach their own personal goals.

Yes, you are the coach. In fact, you epitomize its definition!

"Give a man a fish and you feed him for a day. Teach a man to fish and you feed him for a lifetime." – Chinese Proverb

APPENDIX – MANUAL CALCULATION FORMS

For those of you who are not familiar with Excel spreadsheets, all the calculations discussed in this training module can also be done manually. Simply print the forms on the following pages and follow the instructions.

Excel is a very common business software program. It is highly recommended that you take the time to learn the basics. Not only will you find that it can make your life much easier, you will find it to be a very profitable business tool as well.

Sales Meeting Agenda
Worksheet

Enter data in the yellow boxes to create your Sales Meeting Agenda

Title

Purpose

Date

Start Time	End Time	Duration	Presenter	Discussion Topic

Total

One on One Meeting Planner

Enter information in the yellow boxes to create your One on One Meeting Planner

Sales Representative	
Date	
Date of Next Meeting	

Expected Sales To Close Before Next Meeting

Company	Plan of Action	Purpose of Call

Follow-up On Hot Prospects Before Next Meeting

Company	Plan of Action	Purpose of Call

Action Items to Be Completed Before The Next Meeting

Action Item	Plan of Action	To Be Completed By

Other Objectives, Comments, and To-Do's

Activity Tracking Worksheet

Your average commission rate (Total Commissions Earned / Total Volume of Sales Closed)
Your average size sale (Total Volume of Sales Closed / Total Number of Sales Closed)

The number of presentations it takes you to make a sale (Total Number of Presentations / Total number of Sales Closed)

The number of fact finds it takes you to make a presentation (Total Number of Fact Finds / Total Number of Presentations)

The number of prospecting calls it takes you to book a fact find (Total Number of Prospecting Calls / Total number of Fact Finds)

Week Number	Number of Prospecting Calls Completed	Number of Fact Finds Completed	Number of Presentations Completed	Number of Sales Closed	Volume of Sales Closed	Commissions Earned
1						
2						
3						
4						
5						
6						
7						
8						
9						
10						
11						
12						
13						
14						
15						
16						
17						
18						
19						
20						
21						
22						
23						
24						
25						
26						
27						
28						
29						
30						
31						
32						
33						
34						
35						
36						
37						
38						
39						
40						
41						
42						
43						
44						
45						
46						
47						
48						
49						
50						
51						
52						
Totals						

Sales Funnel
Prospects

Company	Last Step of the Sales Process Completed?	Value of Potential Sale

Sales Funnel Management Worksheet

Your Monthly Sales Objective

The number of presentations it takes you to make a sale

The number of fact finds it takes you to make a presentation

Sales Funnel Targets	Sales Process Step	Sales Funnel Actuals
$ - (Your Monthly Value for Presentations Below X The Number of Fact Finds to Make a Presentation)	Fact Finds Completed	$ - (The Total of Fact Finds Completed from Sales Funnel Prospects Form)
$ - (Your Monthly Sales Objective X The Number of Presentations to Make a Sale)	Presentations Completed	$ - (The Total of Presentations Completed from Sales Funnel Prospects Form)
$ - (Your Monthy Sales Objective)	Sales Completed	$ - (The Total of Sales Completed from Sales Funnel Prospects Form)

Weekly Sales Activity
Tracking Worksheet

Enter information in the yellow boxes to track and monitor your weekly sales activities.

Sales Representative:		Sales to Date:	
Week Ending:		Balance of Month Forecast:	
Initial Monthly Sales Forecast:		Revised Monthly Sales Forecast:	$0

Activity	Monday	Tuesday	Wednesday	Thursday	Friday	Total	(+/-)
Prospecting: Current Customers							
Goal							
Telemarketing Calls Completed							
Site Visits Completed							
Sub Total Calls Completed							
Prospecting: New Contacts							
Goal							
Telemarketing Calls Completed							
Site Visits Completed							
Sub Total Calls Completed							
Follow-up Callbacks from Prospect List							
Telemarketing Calls Completed							
Site Visits Completed							
Sub Total Calls Completed							
Summary of All Prospecting Activities							
Total of Prospecting Calls							
Goal for Appointments Booked							
Actual Appointments Booked							
Fact Finds Completed							
Goal							
Actual							
Presentations of Offer Completed							
Goal							
Actual							
Sales Closed							
Number of Sales Goal							
Number of Sales Actual							
Sales Goal							
Sales Actual							

Sales Process
Summary Worksheet

Enter information in the yellow boxes to complete your Sales Process Summary Worksheet

Appointments Booked from Prospecting Activities

Company	Date Booked	Date of Appointment	Lead Source	Notes

Fact Finds Completed

Company	Date Completed	Date of Presentation	Product of Interest	Size of Possible Sale

Presentations of Offer Completed

Company	Date Completed	Next Step To Complete Sale	Date of Next Step	Rating of Closing This Month

Sales Closed

Company	Date Completed	Product Sold	Size of Sale	Notes

Sales Funnel and Forecast Worksheet

Enter information in the yellow boxes to track your Sales Funnel and create your Sales Forecast.

| Sales Representative: | | Week Ending: | |

Company	Appointment Booked?	Fact Find Completed?	Presentation of Offer Completed?	Sales Completed?	Product	Size of Sale	% of Closing This Month	Expected Closing Date of Date of Next Step

One on One Meeting Planner

Enter information in the yellow boxes to create your One on One Meeting Planner

Sales Representative	
Date	
Date of Next Meeting	

Expected Sales To Close This Week

Company	Plan of Action	Purpose of Call

Follow-up On Hot Prospects This Week

Company	Plan of Action	Purpose of Call

Action Items to Be Completed This Week

Action Item	Plan of Action	To Be Completed By

Other Objectives, Comments, and To-Do's

Next Week's Appointment Calendar

Enter information in the yellow boxes to your weekly appointments.				

Sales Representative:	Sam Sales Rep		Week Ending:	Friday, July 31, 2009

Time	Monday	Tuesday	Wednesday	Thursday	Friday
Date	27-Jul-09	28-Jul-09	29-Jul-09	30-Jul-09	31-Jul-09
7:00 AM					
7:30 AM					
8:00 AM					
8:30 AM					
9:00 AM					
9:30 AM					
10:00 AM					
10:30 AM					
11:00 AM					
11:30 AM					
12:00 PM					
12:30 PM					
1:00 PM					
1:30 PM					
2:00 PM					
2:30 PM					
3:00 PM					
3:30 PM					
4:00 PM					
4:30 PM					
5:00 PM					
5:30 PM					
6:00 PM					
6:30 PM					
7:00 PM					

To Do List	To Do List	To Do List	To Do List	To Do List

**Personal Goal Definition
Worksheet**

Enter information in yellow boxes to define your personal goals.

Step 1 - Personal Commitment

I am committed to and will work towards achieving my personal goals as listed below.

Name	
Date	

Step 2 - Lifestyle & Leisure Time Goals

Next 12 Months	
Next 2 - 4 Years	
Long Term	

Step 3 - Career & Educational Goals

Next 12 Months	
Next 2 - 4 Years	
Long Term	

Step 4 - Health & Fitness Goals

Next 12 Months	
Next 2 - 4 Years	
Long Term	

Step 5 - Spirtual & Community Involvement Goals

Next 12 Months	
Next 2 - 4 Years	
Long Term	

Step 6 - Financial Goals

Next 12 Months	
Next 2 - 4 Years	
Long Term	

Goal Setting & Action Planning Worksheet

1. What is the total annual income you wish to earn to fund your lifestyle?
2. What is your base salary?
3. What is your average monthly bonus earned?
4. Amount of commission income required to reach annual income goal. (#1-(#2 + #3))
5. What is your average commission rate?
6. Total annual sales volume required. ((#4 / #5) x 100)
7. Monthly sales volume required. (#6 / 12)
8. What is you average size of sale?
9. Total number of sales required per month. (#7 / #8)
10. Total number of sales required per week. (#9 / 4)
11. How many presentations does it take you to make a sale?
12. Number of presentations required per month. (#9 x #11)
13. Number of presentations required per week. (#12 / 4)
14. How many fact finds does it take you to make a presentation?
15. Number of fact finds required per month. (#13 x #14)
16. Number of fact finds required per week. (#15 / 4)
17. How many prospecting calls does it take you to book a fact find?
18. Number of prospecting calls required per month. (#15 x #17)
19. Number of prospecting calls required per week. (#18 / 4)
20. Number of prospecting calls required per day. (#19 / 5)

Sales Performance Review & Action Planning Worksheet

Enter information in yellow boxes to complete the worksheet.

Sales Representative:	
Sales Manager:	
Date:	

Section 1 - Previous Time Period's Sales Performance Review

Objective	Goal	Actual	Percentage Attainment

Section 2 - Action Planning

Objective	Recommended Action	Support & Resources Needed	Measurements of Success	Time Frame

Section 3 - Comments

Sales Manager Comments

Sales Represenative Comments

Representative's Signature:		Manager's Signature:	

Minimum Selling Price
Calculation Worksheet

Enter data in the yellow boxes to calculate a product's minimum selling price.

Requested Discounted Selling Price	
Subtract the Cost of Goods Sold	
Subtract Commissions To Be Paid on Sale At Requested Price	
Gross Profit Contibution to Fixed Costs	

Minimum Product Selling Price (Cost of Goods Sold + Commissions +$1)

SAMPLE TERMINATION OF EMPLOYMENT WITHIN PROBATIONARY PERIOD LETTER

August 7, 2009

Samual A. Representative
123 Any Street
Toronto, ON
H0H 0H0

> **Disclaimer**: Always check with legal counsel before using this template to insure you comply with your local labour & employment requirements.

Dear Sam:

This letter will serve to confirm our meeting today during which we advised you of the termination of your employment with _____. This is in accordance with the three-month introductory period clause as outlined in your offer of employment dated _____.

Your employment is terminated effective immediately and you will be paid up to and including today. We will compensate you for any vacation pay or qualifying business expenses that may remain owing to you as of your last day. Any employment separation paperwork that is required will be mailed to you.

You must immediately return all property to which you agreed were to be returned to the company upon request or termination of employment. This includes but is not limited to access cards, keys and computer related equipment. For the assets that you do not have with you now, we trust that you will ensure their safe return to us as soon as possible.

We wish you the very best in your career transition efforts.

Sincerely,

Matthew Manager
Regional Sales Manager

CC: Human Resources Department

SAMPLE 60 DAY WARNING LETTER

August 7, 2009

Samual A. Representative
123 Any Street
Toronto, ON
H0H 0H0

> **Disclaimer**: Always check with legal counsel before using this template to insure you comply with your local labour & employment requirements.

Dear Sam:

As discussed in our meeting today, your sales performance over the past three months is below the required standards and must be corrected immediately.

Specifically, your sales performance is as follows:

- May Sales Results - $43,500 versus quota of $83,333 or 52% attainment
- June Sales Results - $36,750 versus quota of $83,333 or 44% attainment
- July Sales Results – $59,360 versus quota of $83,333 or 71% attainment

Currently, your sales results year to date are only 63% of your assigned quota.

The following are my observations as to why your sales performance is below the required standards:

- Your weekly sales reports indicate that you are averaging only 5 prospecting calls per day, however most sales representatives need an average of at least 10 calls per day to succeed.
- You do not have sufficient sales that are forecasted at 75% or higher to close in any given month to reach quota. Most sales representatives need three times quota or $250,000 forecasted to succeed

As a result of your sales performance falling below 80% year to date, the following Action Plan is being initiated to bring your sales performance up to company standards. This program will remain in place for 30 day increments and will be reviewed with you monthly. These monthly reviews will indicate whether program continuance is warranted. My expectation of your performance and your goal should be achievement of 100% or higher of your assigned quota. This expected performance standard is no more or no less than is expected of any other sales representative.

The components of the Action Plan we are initiating for you are as follows:

You will report to me, weekly on Monday mornings at 8:00 am for a review of your activities of the week. This analysis will consist of:

- Reviewing your week's objectives and accomplishments in terms of sales activities
- Reviewing the new prospects found in your territory
- Reviewing your existing prospects in terms of progression through the sales process.
- Reviewing the growth in the prospects on your sales forecast ranked at 75% or higher of closing within the current month.

Minimum sales activity targets that must be met by you are as follows:

- Complete a minimum of 10 prospecting calls per day.
- Conduct of minimum of 1 fact find appointment per day
- Attend all team meetings and training sessions

Sam, your desire to succeed is critical to you achieving your goals. I am available to assist your efforts.   If you have any questions, do not hesitate to ask.   We will meet again 30 days on September 7, 2009 to discuss your progress.

Failure to meet the targets mentioned above and to successfully improve and sustain your performance could result in further corrective action, up to and including termination of employment.

Please sign below to acknowledge that the contents of this letter have been reviewed with you.

Sincerely,

Matthew Manager
Regional Sales Manager

_____   _____

Employee Signature   Date

CC: Human Resources Department

SAMPLE 30 DAY WARNING LETTER

August 7, 2009

Samual A. Representative
123 Any Street
Toronto, ON
H0H 0H0

> **Disclaimer**: Always check with legal counsel before using this template to insure you comply with your local labour & employment requirements.

Dear Sam:

As discussed in our meeting of August 7, 2009 and again today, your sales performance continues to be below the required standards and must be corrected immediately.

Specifically, your sales performance is as follows:
- June Sales Results - $36,750 versus quota of $83,333 or 44% attainment
- July Sales Results – $59,360 versus quota of $83,333 or 71% attainment
- August Sales Results - $47,620 versus quota of $83,333 or 57% attainment

Currently, your sales results year to date are only 56% of your assigned quota.

The following are my observations as to why your sales performance is below the required standards:
- Your weekly sales reports indicate that you are averaging only 7 prospecting calls per day versus the required minimum of 10.
- You are averaging only 3 fact finds per week versus the required minimum of 1 per day.

As your sales performance has not improved, the Action Plan initiated to bring your sales performance up to company standards on August 7 2009 will continue. My expectation of your performance and your goal should be achievement of 100% or higher of your assigned quota.

I am available to assist your efforts.   If you have any questions, do not hesitate to ask. We will meet again 30 days on October 7, 2009 to discuss your progress.

Failure to meet the targets mentioned above and to successfully improve and sustain your performance could result in further corrective action, up to and including termination of employment.

Please sign below to acknowledge that the contents of this letter have been reviewed with you.

Sincerely,

Matthew Manager
Regional Sales Manager

_____   _____
Employee Signature   Date

CC: Human Resources Department

SAMPLE TERMINATION OF EMPLOYMENT AFTER PROBATIONARY PERIOD LETTER

August 7, 2009

Samual A. Representative
123 Any Street
Toronto, ON H0H 0H0

> **Disclaimer**: Always check with legal counsel before using this template to insure you comply with your local labour & employment requirements.

Dear Sam:

This letter will serve to confirm our meeting today during which we advised you of the termination of your employment with _____. As discussed and confirmed to you in writing on _____ and _____, your sales performance is below company standards, and is the cause for your termination.

Your employment is terminated effective immediately, and you will be paid up to and including _____. This is the equivalent to _____ weeks pay in lieu of termination notice, and is in accordance with our legal requirements.

We will compensate you for any unused vacation pay as legally required, as well as any qualifying business expenses that may remain owing to you as of your last day. Your group benefits will continue for a period of _____ days. Any employment separation paperwork that is required will be mailed to you.

You must immediately return all property to which you agreed were to be returned to the company upon request or termination of employment. This includes but is not limited to access cards, keys and computer related equipment. For the assets that you do not have with you now, we trust that you will ensure their safe return to us as soon as possible.

We wish you the very best in your career transition efforts.

Sincerely,

Matthew Manager
Regional Sales Manager

CC: Human Resources Department

About The Author

"Those who say it cannot be done are
usually interrupted by those already doing it."
- James Baldwin

SUSAN A. ENNS

Susan is a Managing Partner of B2B Sales Connections, having been
with the firm since inception. She brings over 22 years of direct
sales, management and executive level business to business
experience.

Before co-founding B2B Sales Connections, Susan gained marketing,
sales and general management experience in the business
technology and office equipment industries. She also has experience
in the group insurance industry, as well as owning and operating her
own businesses. Some of her career highlights include:

- Directed two regional sales operations simultaneously to outstanding sales growth
- Increased a regional sales operation to 39% average annual sales growth over a 5
  year period
- Achieved 374% of profit targets as Branch Manager
- Managed the top branch in Canada, with consistent year over year record sales
  results
- Operation selected as a finalist in the Better Business Bureau Torch Awards for
  Marketplace Ethics
- Sales Representative of the Year for two consecutive years before being promoted to
  sales management

Susan has received her Bachelor of Commerce (Honours) degree from the Faculty of
Management at the University of Manitoba, where she was named to the Dean's Honour
List in three separate years. She is also a Certified Internal ISO Auditor.

She has written the training courses for sales and sales management, created numerous
automated sales tools, and as the B2B Sales Coach, she writes and edits the company's
newsletters. Her work has been published in several locations numerous times and has
sold on four separate continents.

For many years, Susan has volunteered on numerous executive committees of professional associations, sport leagues and clubs in which she has been a member. Participating on the Leadership Executive of the Sales Professionals of Ottawa since 2008, she has served as Marketing Lead, Vice President, and is currently the association's President. She has also been a guest lecturer at the School of Business at Algonquin College as well as a guest speaker for SPO. She is an annual participant in the Canadian Cancer Society Relay for Life, and holds multiple positions on the Volunteer Committee for the Canadian Breast Cancer Foundation CIBC Run For The Cure.

A competitive athlete from an early age, she is a Kinsmen Award Winner for Good Citizenship, Sportsmanship, and Hard Work. Now an avid golfer, she has been voted Most Sportsmanlike Player and All Star Skip in separate curling leagues.

By creating and teaching various sales training courses, coupled with the innovative creation and implementation of useful sales tools, Susan has excelled and been recognized in all areas of her personal and professional endeavors.

Other Titles from Susan A. Enns

Discover these titles from Susan A. Enns, Managing Partner of B2B Sales Connections at www.b2bsalesconnections.com

- Action Plan For Sales Success
- Action Plan For Sales Management Success
- Daily Motivational Quotes

Connect with Susan Online

Connect with Susan online at

- Website: www.b2bsalesconnections.com
- A Sales Compass: A Blog by B2B Sales Connections: www.b2bscblog.com
- LinkedIn: www.linkedin.com/in/SusanEnns
- Facebook: www.facebook.com/B2BSalesConnections
- Twitter: www.twitter.com/SusanEnns
- YouTube: www.youtube.com/SusanEnns
- Skype: User Name - susanenns.14

www.ingramcontent.com/pod-product-compliance
Lightning Source LLC
Chambersburg PA
CBHW080330270326
41927CB00014B/3167